"By correctly fra   dvent of Christ, *A Savi*   ncarnation while avc   srep-resent the Christmas story. Each chapter is not only theologically rich but also practically beneficial. Pastors and congregants alike will find these pages immeasurably helpful."

—**Adam B. Dooley**, pastor, Englewood
Baptist Church, Jackson, Tennessee

"My long-time friend, Dr. Bill Cook, has written a masterful work about the Lord Jesus. *A Savior is Born* is scholarly, devotional, practical, and missional. Dr. Cook exegetes and explains the birth narratives and describes a Jesus worthy of our worship, following, and obedience in taking the message of Jesus to all the nations."

—**Robin Jumper**, executive vice president of
academic affairs, Baptist University of Florida

"*A Savior is Born* expounds the thirteen central passages that directly relate to the Christmas story as well an Old Testament biblical theology of messianic expectations. This invaluable resource is written for veteran preachers and teachers, parents leading children in family worship, and even new Christians. I thank God for this important resource."

—**Brian Payne**, Lakeview Baptist Church, Auburn, Alabama

"Dr. Cook provides a rich meditation on the beginning of Christ's life that complements his previous volume, *Jesus's Final Week*. The text features careful interaction with numerous scriptural texts, suggested personal reflections, and even Christmas hymns. This work provides readers not only with a greater knowledge about the early events in Christ's life, but it will also, through the work of the Spirit, cause moments of reflection that can engender personal transformation."

—**David Rathel**, associate professor of Christian
theology and director of academic graduate
studies program, Gateway Seminary

"Bill Cook's *A Savior is Born* is rich in Scriptures and deep in meaning. The work is a challenge to all who find themselves busy in life to not overlook the significance of the coming of Christ. Bill reminds us that this very event was the eternal plan of God, and that this event is a demonstration of his love for us. I found myself challenged to understand in a fresh way the significance of the coming of Christ and to a constant state of worship!"

—**L. Thomas Strong III**, vice president of spiritual formation and student life, dean of students and professor of New Testament and Greek, New Orleans Baptist Theological Seminary

"Dr. Bill Cook taught me how to teach the Bible theologically. As a seminary student, I took a class from him on the Gospel of John and benefited from years of sitting under his theologically rich preaching as my pastor. In *A Savior is Born*, Dr. Cook skillfully presents a clear, detailed, and profound theological analysis of key biblical passages surrounding the birth of Jesus. For many of us, familiarity with these texts often leads us to a mere cursory reading. Dr. Cook invites readers to rediscover the profound truths they proclaim. This book not only provides fresh insights but also guides readers to recognize the theological depth of these passages and respond to the message with renewed faith and worship. As a pastor and scholar, Dr. Cook leverages his remarkable gifts and extensive experience to skillfully shepherd readers through the most important event in human history, Jesus's birth."

—**Keith S. Whitfield**, associate professor of theology, Southeastern Baptist Theological Seminary

A SAVIOR

is BORN

A SAVIOR
IS BORN

From
HEAVEN'S THRONE
to **BETHLEHEM'S MANGER**

WILLIAM F. COOK III

ACADEMIC®
BRENTWOOD, TENNESSEE

I dedicate this book to Jaylynn, the most wonderful person I have ever known. Thank you for your love for me, our family, and our church. No one has had a greater influence in my life for godliness than you. Your passion for Jesus is a daily reminder to me that Jesus matters most! Your love for the Christ of Christmas reminds me that the person of Jesus matters more than all the ornaments and presents of the holiday season. Yet you make each Christmas season more wonderful than the one before. I love you!

CONTENTS

ACKNOWLEDGMENTS

I am grateful for Dr. R. Albert Mohler, president of The Southern Baptist Theological Seminary; Dr. Paul Akin, provost; and Dr. Hershael York, dean of the School of Theology, for a sabbatical leave from my teaching responsibilities to work on this volume. I am also extremely grateful for the kind folks at B&H Academic for giving me the privilege of writing this book. They have been very patient, kind, and helpful to me along the way. I would be amiss not to mention the staff at The Ninth and O Baptist Church for their willingness to allow me to occasionally miss our staff meetings to focus extra attention on my writing and for their prayers for me. Thank you!

PREFACE

Christmas is God's yearly reminder for sinners to come out of the darkness and into the light. During the Christmas season, even those who don't know Jesus love the lights and songs of Christmas. While most people seldom pause to listen carefully to the words of the traditional Christmas carols, those who do pause will hear praise to God for the gift of Jesus. Occasionally, the truths in these carols find a way into people's hearts. For many people, after the presents are opened and the gifts carefully stored away, there is a sense of emptiness, a longing for something more. The thought resonates in the minds of many, "Is this all there is?" Unfortunately, for most people, that *is* all there is. Sadly enough, even for many Christians who genuinely love Jesus, the holiday noise drowns out the true meaning of the season.

Jesus Christ is the most important person in human history. Those who call him Savior and Lord believe him to be God incarnate. Jesus existed before he was conceived in Mary's womb, but once conceived he became one of us, except for our sinful nature. The good news of Christmas is that Jesus came to save sinners like you and me. Christmas testifies to God's love for us and his commitment to save a people for his own possession. While I hope this book is instructive, I pray it is also transformational. We need to know the truth about Jesus's coming, but we need to be transformed by that truth as well. Ultimately, transformation is the work of the Holy Spirit. However, the Spirit of God uses the Word of God to transform the people of God into the image of the Son of God. That transformation is my prayer for you as you read this book.

Because the Spirit and Word work together, I have included many Bible verses, some of which are printed out for you in the text. I am convinced that too many of us pass over the Scripture references in the books we read without looking them up. By incorporating them into the text, my hope is that you will see how the Bible is a book about Jesus. This is especially true in the Birth and Infancy narratives and their abundant references to the Old Testament.

This book serves as a bookend to my earlier work, *Jesus's Final Week*.[1] The two volumes bracket the life of Christ. This volume is longer and more detailed. The reason for this is that in my previous work I had to summarize a significant portion of the Gospels. The Gospels spend approximately 40 percent of their space on Jesus's final days. This many verses required me to paint with broader strokes. The Birth and Infancy narratives are confined almost exclusively to Matthew 1 and 2 and Luke 1 and 2, and this allows me to dig down a little deeper. The audience of the book is my first-year seminary students and those seated in the seats of The Ninth and O Baptist Church. I have taught New Testament at The Southern Baptist Theological Seminary since 2000 and served as lead pastor of The Ninth and O Baptist Church since 2001. Serving in these two capacities has made me a better professor by continually reminding

---

[1] William F. Cook III, *Jesus's Final Week: From Triumphal Entry to Empty Tomb* (Nashville: B&H Academic, 2022).

me that I am preparing students for Christ's church, and it has made me a better pastor by allowing me time to go deeper in my studies.

Gloria in excelsis Deo,
Bill Cook

INTRODUCTION

The New Testament opens with a statement linking Jesus to both Abraham and David (Matt 1:1). Abraham and David are two of the most titanic figures in the Hebrew Scriptures. Matthew's opening lines point to Jesus as "the seed of Abraham" and the "Son of David." The other Gospels begin their work in their own way. John begins his Gospel by taking his readers back before the beginning of time (John 1:1). The Gospel of John boldly declares that Jesus, the *Logos*, is preexistent, equal to God, and the Creator of all things (1:1–3). John may have thought that his readers could not make sense of Jesus's story without understanding his deity. Luke, on the other hand, wanted his readers to understand that his Gospel was the result of painstaking research (Luke 1:1–4). As we will soon see, it is possible that Luke spoke to Mary and gleaned much of his information from her. The Gospel of Mark, on the other hand, begins with the words, "The beginning of the gospel of Jesus Christ" (Mark 1:1). For Mark, the beginning begins with John the Baptist, the forerunner of Jesus. While the four evangelists begin their Gospels in their own way, each Gospel makes clear that Jesus the Messiah is the central figure.

Differing Perspectives

Only Matthew and Luke provide readers with information about Jesus's birth and infancy. Matthew's and Luke's accounts overlap at certain points but differ at times as well. These differences are the result of each telling the same story from different perspectives. Another way to state the matter is that their accounts are complementary rather than contradictory. Matthew and Luke each recount key events that they deemed important for their readers. Matthew and Luke were theologians as well as historians.

Matthew's account is told from Joseph's perspective, while Luke's account is told from Mary's perspective. In Matthew, an angel appeared to Joseph to announce the virginal conception, while in Luke the angel Gabriel appeared to Mary (Matt 1:18–25; Luke 1:26–38). If one read only Matthew's Gospel, one could get the impression that the entire story began in Bethlehem rather than Nazareth (Matt 2:1). The Gospel of Matthew explains why the family fled Bethlehem and traveled to Egypt, then settled in Nazareth (Matt 2:13–23). The Gospel of Luke, on the other hand, describes how Joseph and Mary began in Nazareth and then traveled to Bethlehem (Luke 2:1–7). Matthew begins his Gospel with Jesus's genealogy (Matt 1:1–17); Luke waits until chapter 3 to introduce Jesus's genealogy (Luke 3:23–38). In Matthew, Jesus's genealogy begins with Abraham and works forward to Jesus, while Luke's presentation of Jesus's genealogy begins with Jesus and goes back to Adam. In Matthew, key events are said to fulfill specific Old Testament references, while in Luke the Old Testament Scriptures provide the backdrop for various messianic "songs." In Matthew, Jesus was worshiped by the magi (Matt 2:1–12); while in Luke, Jesus was worshiped by the shepherds (Luke 2:15–20). These matters and many others will be discussed in much more detail in the pages to follow.

While some of these differences seem quite substantial on the surface, the similarities between the two accounts verify the authors are telling the same story from their own perspectives. For example, in both Gospels, Jesus was born in Bethlehem during the days of Herod the Great, and his youth was spent in Nazareth (Matt 2:1, 23; Luke 2:4, 39). In both Gospels, Jesus belongs to the family line of David (Matt 1:1; Luke 1:27). In both Gospels, Mary and Jospeh are said to be engaged (Matt 1:18; Luke 1:27). In both Gospels, Jesus was conceived by the powerful working of the Holy Spirit while Mary was a virgin (Matt 1:18, 25; Luke 1:27, 35). In both Gospels, the name "Jesus" was chosen by God and announced by an angel (Matt 1:21, 31; Luke 1:31). In both Gospels, Jesus's birth was the fulfillment of scriptural promises to Israel. The two accounts are clearly complementary rather than contradictory. The authors carefully selected events they deemed important for their readers to know.

Matthew's Account

While we will examine the material in the following chapters from a chronological perspective, understanding the characteristics in Matthew and Luke, respectively, is important. For example, Matthew's Birth and Infancy narrative is structured around five Old Testament quotations. While Matthew's choice of certain Scriptures may initially seem odd to us, he saw them as being fulfilled in Christ. Second, Matthew informs his readers of Jesus's identity in the first chapter. Jesus is a descendant of Abraham and David, thereby tying him to the Abrahamic and Davidic covenants. He is named "Jesus," and his mission is "to save his people from their sins" (Matt 1:21). Furthermore, he is "Immanuel" ("God is with us") (Matt 1:23). By the time one finishes the first chapter, one knows exactly who Matthew believed Jesus to be. The second chapter focuses attention on the fact that where Jesus lived fulfilled Israel's ancient Scriptures: Bethlehem, Egypt, and Nazareth (Matt 2:6, 13, 23). There are many questions to be answered concerning these matters, and we will look at each one in more detail in subsequent chapters.

Luke's Account

Luke's account has the "feel" of an Old Testament story. Two examples are the angelic announcements of miraculous conceptions and the ancient ceremonies being performed in the Jerusalem temple (Luke 1:5–38; 2:21–24). The Gospel of Luke alternates stories between the birth, circumcision, and naming of John the Baptist and of Jesus. Luke, however, always makes the point that Jesus was superior to John. Those associated with Jesus were faithful followers of Yahweh. Four of those individuals are not mentioned anywhere else in the Gospels: Zechariah, Elizabeth, Simeon, and Anna. Luke intended for his readers to learn from these individuals how to respond to the workings of God. Finally, much of Luke's theology in these chapters can be found in four Messianic "songs": Mary's *Magnificat* (1:46–55), Zechariah's *Benedictus* (1:68–79), the angels' *Gloria* (2:14), and Simeon's *Nunc Dimittis* (2:29–32). These four songs not only punctuate the narrative but also infuse it with a note of prophetic and celebratory joy.

We turn our focus now to Matthew's and Luke's Birth and Infancy narratives. With a few exceptions, I follow the order of events in A. T. Robertson's *A Harmony of the Gospels*.[1] I will attempt to set each passage in its literary context as well as to situate the passages in their chronological setting. The reflections at the end of each chapter are an attempt to briefly consider some of the implications of the text for Christian living. The hymns are intended to be sung to God as acts of worship for the sending of his Son. Finally, I have included some "Deeper Dives" into various theological topics touched on in some passages to show how key themes in the birth stories are expanded throughout the Gospels.

---

[1] A. T. Robertson, *A Harmony of the Gospels for Students of the Life of Christ: Based on the Broadus Harmony in the Revised Version* (New York: Harper & Brothers, 1922).

CHAPTER 1

THE INCARNATION OF GOD'S SON

JOHN 1:1–18

> "In the beginning was the Word, and the Word was with God, and the Word was God."
> —John 1:1

John's prologue may seem like a strange place to begin the first Christmas story. Both the Gospel of Matthew and the Gospel of Luke have Birth and Infancy narratives. The Gospel of John, however, begins before the creation of the world. John helps his readers understand that Jesus existed before he was supernaturally conceived in Mary's womb. In the passage above, John presents the beginning of Jesus's story from above, from a divine perspective. Matthew and Luke tell their Birth and Infancy stories from below, from the perspective of those involved in the events. While both Matthew's and Luke's accounts are theological, John's prologue adds a theological depth unparalleled in the rest of Scripture. John's prologue makes the astonishing claim that Jesus Christ is God and that this reality changes everything.

John wrote his Gospel approximately fifty-five years after Jesus's resurrection.[1] John spent over five decades thinking about Christ's words and deeds. As John contemplated how to begin his Gospel, he determined he had to go back before the beginning of time to tell the story of Jesus. With this passage, we will explore the prologue's connections to the incarnation of Jesus. We will examine how the prologue helps us better understand the meaning of Jesus's arrival in the world, and we will concentrate on the first and last paragraph of the passage, as they are most important for our consideration of Jesus's incarnation.

In the Beginning (1:1–5)

One can hardly imagine a more fascinating opening to a biography than the words, "In the beginning." The phrase hearkens back to the opening words of the Bible, "In the beginning God created the heavens and the earth" (Gen 1:1). If Gen 1:1 describes the beginning of creation, John 1:1 tells the story of the beginning of a new creation.[2]

The opening words of Genesis and John speak to a time before time, a time before anything existed but the Triune God. The most important term in the prologue is "Word" (*logos*). Scholars debate the background of the term, whether its origin

---

[1] On the dating of John's Gospel see D. A. Carson and Douglas J. Moo, *An Introduction to the New Testament* (Grand Rapids: Zondervan, 2005), 264–67.

[2] Jeannine K. Brown, "Creation's Renewal in the Gospel of John," *Catholic Biblical Quarterly* 72 (2010), 275–90.

is Hellenistic philosophy or the Hebrew Scriptures.[3] Because John's prologue mentions creation (vv. 1–5), the tabernacle (v. 14), Moses (v. 17), and the Law (v. 17), we should understand the Hebrew Scriptures as the background to John's use of the term *logos*. Martin Hengel writes concerning the Word, "[It] expresses the eternal being of the Word right from eternity in inseparable communion with God."[4] In the Old Testament, God's word is the dynamic force of his will. Consider the following passages (italics added).

> Then God *said*, "Let there be light," and there was light. (Gen 1:3)

> After these events, *the word of the* LORD *came* to Abram in a vision. (Gen 15:1)

> The heavens were made *by the word* of the LORD, and all the stars, *by the breath of his mouth*. (Ps 33:6)

> "So *my word* that comes from my mouth will not return to me empty, but it will accomplish what I please and will prosper in *what I send it* to do." (Isa 55:11)

John makes four important points about the Word in the opening verses. First, before anything was created, the Word existed. This boldly declares the Word's preexistence (vv. 1a, 2).

---

[3] For a more complete discussion of the term *logos*, see John F. McHugh, *A Critical and Exegetical Commentary on John 1–4*, International Critical Commentary (London, UK: T&T Clark, 2009), 7–9.

[4] Martin Hengel, "The Prologue of the Gospel of John as the Gateway to Christological Truth," in *The Gospel of John in Christian Theology*, ed. Richard Bauckham and Carl Mosser (Grand Rapids: Eerdmans, 2008), 266.

Second, the Word exists in the closest possible relationship with God, but the Word is distinct from God the Father (vv. 1b, 2). Third, John confesses the Word is God (v. 1c). Fourth, the Word is the agent by which God created all things (vv. 3–5).[5]

John's first point is an assertion of the Word's preexistence. The doctrine of Christ's preexistence is not only taught explicitly in the prologue but is also implied in numerous passages in John's Gospel.

> "No one has ascended into heaven except the one who descended from heaven—the Son of Man." (3:13)

> "For the bread of God is the one who comes down from heaven and gives life to the world." (6:33)

> "For I have come down from heaven, not to do my own will, but the will of him who sent me." (6:38)

> "Then what if you were to observe the Son of Man ascending to where he was before?" (6:62)

> "You are from below," he told them, "I am from above. You are of this world; I am not of this world." (8:23)

> Jesus said to them, "Truly I tell you, before Abraham was, I am." (8:58)

> "I came from the Father and have come into the world. Again, I am leaving the world and going to the Father." (16:28)

---

[5] For a discussion on the use of *theos* in relation to Jesus see Murray J. Harris, *Jesus as God: The New Testament Use of* Theos *in Reference to Jesus* (Eugene, OR: Wipf & Stock, 2008).

John's claims are astounding, especially considering the fact that these verses refer to one born in Bethlehem and placed in a manger. The baby Jesus was God incarnate, who existed before all things and is creator of all things. Even more astonishing is the fact that he created the very woman within whom he was supernaturally conceived. Our familiarity with John's prologue can cause us to miss its majestic glory. The Eternal One became a human being, the God-man. John states the matter even more boldly in v. 14, "The Word became flesh and dwelt among us." John is saying the one thing that cannot be said in polite company: Jesus Christ is God. Contemporary people are happy to talk about a baby in a manger, but to declare him to be God incarnate is blasphemous to the modern mind. Yet the fact that Jesus Christ is God is the very thing we must say, especially when we celebrate his birth. The apostle Paul stated in Col 1:15–16,

> He [Christ] is the image of the invisible God,
> the firstborn over all creation.
> For everything was created by him,
> in heaven and on earth,
> the visible and the invisible,
> whether thrones or dominions
> or rulers or authorities—
> all things have been created through him and for him.

Paul's statement—that all things were created by Jesus and for Jesus—brings much clarity to the meaning of our own lives. We owe our existence to Jesus, and we find our purpose in living for him.

In v. 5, John understood the incarnation to have initiated a cosmic battle between light and darkness, between Jesus and Satan, between heaven and hell, and between truth and error.

John's words, "That light shines in the darkness, and yet the darkness did not overcome it" (v. 5) are remarkable.[6] Throughout John's Gospel, we see that Jesus faced intense opposition from the Jerusalem leadership. As John reflected on that opposition, he understood that standing behind those who opposed Jesus was Satan himself. The matter is stated forthrightly in the following passages.

> "You are of your father the devil, and you want to carry out your father's desires. He was a murderer from the beginning and does not stand in the truth, because there is no truth in him. When he tells a lie, he speaks from his own nature, because he is a liar and the father of lies." (8:44)

> Now when it was time for supper, the devil had already put it into the heart of Judas, Simon Iscariot's son, to betray him. (13:2)

> After Judas ate the piece of bread, Satan entered him. So Jesus told him, "What you're doing, do quickly." (13:27)

All of this provides insight into Herod the Great's attempt to kill the newborn "King of the Jews" (Matt 2:13–21; cf. Rev 12:1–6). Herod's killing of the baby boys in Bethlehem was the darkness seeking to overpower the light.

Before we leave v. 5, we need to understand that the word *katalambanō* can be translated "overcome" (CSB, ESV) but can also be translated as "grasp" (NASB) or "comprehend" (NKJV).

---

[6] For more on the imagery of light see "Taking a Deeper Dive" at the conclusion of this chapter.

The idea would then be that the darkness did not understand the light. An example would be Nicodemus's confusion of what Jesus meant by being born again (3:1–15). The possibility exists that John intended both ideas to be present.[7] If both thoughts are intended, then John is saying not only did the darkness not overpower the light, but also those in darkness (e.g., Nicodemus) did not comprehend the light (cf. 3:19–21).

As we can see, the opening paragraph of John's Gospel is stunning. The baby born in Bethlehem is the preexistent eternal Son of God. All things have been created by him and for him. Yet he became a helpless baby cuddled in his mother's arms, surrounded by barn animals, and placed in a feeding trough. Clearly God's ways are not our ways.

The Word Became Flesh (1:14–18)

This section of the prologue provides further insight into Jesus's incarnation.[8] Verses 14–18 set forth the idea that the incarnation of the Word is God's climactic revelation of himself to sinful humanity. The author of Hebrews made a similar affirmation in Heb 1:1–4. This important passage reads (italics added),

---

[7] Gary M. Burge, *John*, NIV Application Commentary (Grand Rapids: Zondervan, 2000), 56. For discussions of double entendre in John see Andreas J. Köstenberger, *A Theology of John's Gospel and Letters*, Biblical Theology of the New Testament, ed. Andreas J. Köstenberger (Grand Rapids: Zondervan, 2009), 132; Earl J. Richard, "Expressions of Double Meaning and Their Function in the Gospel of John," 31 no. 1 (1985), 96–112.

[8] This section is drawing on my discussion found in William F. Cook III, *John: Jesus Christ Is God*, Focus on the Bible (Scotland, UK: Christian Focus, 2016), 20–23.

Long ago God spoke to our ancestors by the prophets at different times and in different ways. In these last days, he has *spoken* to us by his Son. God has appointed him heir of all things and *made the universe through him.* The Son is the radiance of God's glory and the exact expression of his nature, sustaining all things by his powerful word. After making purification for sins, he sat down at the right hand of the Majesty on high. So he became superior to the angels, just as the name he inherited is more excellent than theirs.

The author of Hebrews, just as John did in his prologue, associated Jesus with creation, with God's glory, and with the revelation of God's nature. In v. 17, Jesus is specifically identified with the *logos*, "for the law was given through Moses; grace and truth came through Jesus Christ." These verses are the culmination of John's thinking on the significance of Jesus's coming into the world.

In a very real sense, v. 14 is the high point of human history: "The Word became flesh and dwelt among us. We observed his glory, the glory as the one and only Son from the Father, full of grace and truth." John chose to use the term "flesh" (*sarx*) to communicate the full humanity of Jesus. Jesus took on human flesh with all its frailty, except for indwelling sin. When Jesus became tired, he needed to rest. If he was hit, he would bruise. If he was pierced on a cross, he would bleed and experience excruciating pain. Paul stated in Phil 2:5–8,

Adopt the same attitude as that of Christ Jesus,
who, existing in the form of God,
did not consider equality with God
as something to be exploited.
Instead he emptied himself

by assuming the form of a servant,
taking on the likeness of humanity.
And when he had come as a man,
he humbled himself by becoming obedient
to the point of death—
even to death on a cross.

When Paul wrote that Jesus existed in "the form of God," he was not saying that Jesus only *seemed* to be God but that he *is* God. The point Philippians makes is that Jesus did not use his deity to his own advantage. Rather than exploiting his divine power, he took on human flesh and became an obedient servant of God. Jesus's obedient service led him to a cross, where he demonstrated for everyone the truth: the first is to be last, and the greatest is to become the servant of all (Mark 10:31, 44).

For John to say that Jesus "became" (*ginomai*) flesh suggests that prior to his incarnation, he did not have a body. Most fascinating of all is the fact that he "dwelt" among those whom he created. Jesus did not perform his salvific work from a distance, but he came up close and personal to those he created and came to redeem. The word translated "dwelt" (*skēnoō*) means "pitched his tent" or "tabernacled" among us.[9] In the Old Testament, the tabernacle was the place where God dwelt among his people (Exod 25:8–9; Ezek 43:7) and manifested his Shekinah glory (*doxa*) to them.[10] God's glory is now manifested in the Father's one and only Son. Isaiah prophesied of a day when God's glory

---

[9] Colin G. Kruse, *John*, Tyndale New Testament Commentaries (Downers Grove: IVP Academic, 2003), 69.

[10] On the theme of glory in John's Gospel see Richard Bauckham, *Gospel of Glory: Major Themes in Johannine Theology* (Grand Rapids: Baker Academic, 2015), 43–62.

would be revealed to all people (Isa 40:5; 60:1–2). These two key
passages are:

> And the glory of the LORD will appear,
> and all humanity together will see it,
> for the mouth of the LORD has spoken. (Isa 40:5)

> Arise, shine, for your light has come,
> and the glory of the LORD shines over you.
> For look, darkness will cover the earth,
> and total darkness the peoples;
> but the LORD will shine over you,
> and his glory will appear over you. (Isa 60:1–2)

John implies a fulfillment of Isaiah's promise in reference to
Jesus's incarnation when he wrote, "We observed his glory"
(1:14).[11] John's use of glory is interesting since he is the only
evangelist not to describe the manifestation of Jesus's glory on
the Mount of Transfiguration. In the Fourth Gospel, God's glory
in Christ is seen in Jesus's signs (miracles) and in his crucifixion,
resurrection, and ascension.

> Jesus did this, the first of his signs, in Cana of Galilee. He
> revealed his glory, and his disciples believed in him. (2:11)

> When Jesus heard it, he said, "This sickness will not end
> in death but is for the glory of God, so that the Son of
> God may be glorified through it." (11:4)

---

[11] On the influence of Isaiah in John's Gospel see Catrin H. Williams,
"Johannine Christology and Prophetic Traditions: The Case of Isaiah," in
Reading the Gospel of John's Christology as Jewish Messianism, ed. Benjamin
E. Reynolds and Gabriele Boccaccini (Leiden, NL: Brill, 2018), especially
92–123.

Jesus said to her, "Didn't I tell you that if you believed you would see the glory of God?" (11:40)

John understood Jesus's crucifixion, resurrection, and ascension as a single event that brings glory to God:

> He [Jesus] said this about the Spirit. Those who believed in Jesus were going to receive the Spirit, for the Spirit had not yet been given because Jesus had not yet been glorified. (7:39)

> His disciples did not understand these things at first. However, when Jesus was glorified, then they remembered that these things had been written about him and that they had done these things to him. (12:16)

> Isaiah said these things because he saw his glory and spoke about him. (12:41)

The world's glory consists in glitz and glitter, neon lights and impressive resumes. God's glory, however, is manifested in a crucified, risen, and exalted Savior.

Reminding ourselves of the purpose of this discussion may be helpful. John's prologue offers insight into the first Christmas story, which is paramount if we are to grasp the depth of what took place in Bethlehem. The baby born in Bethlehem was no ordinary Jewish baby. The baby was none other than God in human flesh. The Gospel of John refers to Jesus as God's "one and only Son" (*monogenēs*), that is, Jesus is God's Son in a way no other person is (v. 14, 18).[12]

---

[12] On the superiority of *monogenēs* being translated "one and only" instead of "only begotten" (KJV) see Kruse, *John*, 70–72.

Why does John the apostle bring John the Baptist back into the discussion here (v. 15)? The Baptist is first mentioned in vv. 6–9. The apostle likely inserts the Baptist here for two reasons.[13] First, what the apostle has just said about the Word is almost too incredible to believe. The Baptist provides a second witness to the apostle's comments (Deut 17:6; 19:15). Second, as the apostle prepares to identify the Word as Jesus, we must remember that John the Baptist prepared the way for the coming of Jesus.

Verses 16 and 17 return to the words of the apostle John and focus attention on the grace Jesus bestows on his people ("grace upon grace"). Considering v. 17, we should understand John's thought to be that the grace of Christ replaces the grace of the law ("grace instead of grace").[14] John is not speaking disparagingly of the Old Covenant mediated through Moses but accentuating the greatness of the New Covenant mediated through Jesus Christ.[15] A theme that will be clearer in Matthew's Birth and Infancy narrative is that Jesus is a second and greater Moses.

The final verse of the passage returns to the central truth of the prologue: the incarnate Jesus is God ("The one and only Son, who is himself God"). When John writes that no one "has

---

[13] Cook, *John*, 22.

[14] The translation "grace upon grace" can suggest the idea of accumulation. The translation of "grace instead of grace" carries the thought of replacement. The thought of accumulation is favored by Craig S. Keener, *The Gospel of John: A Commentary*, 2 vols. (Peabody, MA: Hendrickson, 2003), 1:421. The thought of replacement is favored by D. A. Carson, *The Gospel According to John*, The Pillar New Testament Commentary (Grand Rapids: Eerdmans, 1991), 132.

[15] Cook, *John*, 22.

ever seen God," John is conveying the truth that no one has seen God's divine fullness. God revealed himself to his people in various ways in the Old Testament (Heb 1:1–4). For example, while both Moses and Isaiah saw a portion of God's glorious presence, neither saw the fullness of God's glorious presence (Exod 33:17–23; Isa 6:1–5).[16] But if anyone wants to know what God is like, he merely must read the Gospels where Jesus is the perfect revelation of God. The invisible God (the Father) is made visible in the person of his Son (John 1:18). John's prologue adds a theological depth to the first story of Christmas that is not often considered during the Christian celebration of Christmas.

Final Reflections

One wonders where to begin when seeking to highlight important themes from John 1:1–18. The focus of our attention will be on what I believe is the most important teaching in the prologue—Jesus Christ is God. The church of the twenty-first century must recapture a vision of Jesus. The Jesus many worship is far too small. The shallow Christology of many churches is evident in the weak and anemic singing that takes place on Sunday mornings. A Christian's failure to be committed to faithfully attending their local church demonstrates a shallow understanding of who Jesus is. We must recognize that our hesitancy to advance the gospel across the street and around the world reflects an insufficient view of the incarnation. Jesus left the glories of heaven to descend into a fallen world to bring salvation to sinners. At Christmas, too many believers worship a baby in a manger rather than a King on his throne. When we consider

---

[16] Cook, 22.

that "the Word became flesh and dwelt among us," we have no excuse for not sacrificing time, money, and energy to advance the gospel to the ends of the earth. Those who attend worship only on Christmas and Easter clearly worship a Jesus that does not exist, for when one catches a glimpse of the Jesus presented in John's prologue, the response will be, "Here I am, Lord, send me!" Therefore, Christmas is a time for the deepening of our worship and a recommitment to world evangelization.

A Christmas Hymn of Response

Come, Thou long-expected Jesus,
Born to set Thy people free;
From our fears and sins release us;
Let us find our rest in Thee.
Israel's strength and consolation,
Hope of all the earth Thou art;
Dear desire of every nation,
Joy of every longing heart.

Born Thy people to deliver,
Born a child, and yet a King,
Born to reign in us forever,
Now Thy gracious kingdom bring.
By Thine own eternal spirit
Rule in all our hearts alone;
By Thine all-sufficient merit,
Raise us to Thy glorious throne.[17]

---

[17] Charles Wesley, "Come, Thou Long-Expected Jesus," 1744, *Baptist Hymnal*, #77.

Taking a Deeper Dive: The Imagery of Light

From an earthly perspective, darkness can be frightening. People get lost at night and in the dark can trip over unseen objects. The bedrooms of many children are illuminated by the reassuring presence of a nightlight. The cover of darkness is a prime time for criminal activity. Villains are often associated with darkness. Seasons of grief and mourning have been described as the "Dark Night of the Soul." Little wonder people so highly value the reassuring illumination of light.

The imagery of light plays an important role in the Old Testament. In the creation narrative, God's first creative act was the creation of light. Before God created the sun, moon, and stars, he created light. The heavenly luminaries were not created until the fourth day of creation (Gen 1:14–19). On the first day of creation God said:

> "Let there be light," and there was light. God saw that the light was good, and God separated the light from the darkness. God called the light "day," and the darkness he called "night." There was an evening, and there was a morning: one day. (Gen 1:3–5)

Light imagery is highlighted in Israel's exodus from Egypt. For example, when God brought Israel out of Egyptian bondage, "The LORD went ahead of them in a pillar of cloud to lead them on their way during the day and in a pillar of fire to give them light at night, so that they could travel day or night" (Exod 13:21). In Ps 119:105, God's Word is a lamp illuminating one's path ("Your word is a lamp to my feet and a light to my path," ESV). Psalm 130:5–6 compares the heart's longing for God to the sun rising in the sky and dispelling the darkness: "I wait for the Lord; I wait and put my hope in his word. I wait for the Lord more than watchmen for the morning—more than watchmen for the morning."

The symbolism of light and darkness can be found in the prophetic literature as well, especially in the book of Isaiah. Isaiah associates the coming of light with the coming of an anticipated ideal king: "The people walking in darkness have seen a great light; a light has dawned on those living in the land of darkness" (Isa 9:2). This passage is particularly important because Matthew quotes and applies it to Jesus's ministry (Matt 4:16). In the larger context of Isaiah 9, this "great light" shining "in a land of deep darkness" describes the birth of a coming king. This passage is one of the most important Old Testament passages on the coming of Christ the King. The passage reads:

> For a child will be born for us, a son will be given to us, and the government will be on his shoulders. He will be named Wonderful Counselor, Mighty God, Eternal Father, Prince of Peace. The dominion will be vast, and its prosperity will never end. He will reign on the throne of David and over his kingdom, to establish and sustain it with justice and righteousness from now on and forever. The zeal of the Lord of Armies will accomplish this. (Isa 9:6–7)

As the book of Isaiah moves toward its final chapters, light is associated with the glory of God and the city of Jerusalem, the city of the great King. God's glory is his radiant manifest presence. The passage reads, "Arise, shine, for your light has come, and the glory of the Lord shines over you. For look, darkness will cover the earth, and total darkness the peoples; but the Lord will shine over you, and his glory will appear over you. Nations

will come to your light, and kings to your shining brightness"
(Isa 60:1–3). Jerusalem will one day be a city filled with the
glory of God, and the nations of the earth will be drawn to her
because of her brilliant light. The apostle John used this imagery
when he described the beauty of the new Jerusalem descending from heaven. In that place, there will be no more tears, no
more mourning, no more crying and heartache, no more death,
and no more darkness. The beautiful city will have no temple
since the Lord God Almighty and the Lamb will be present
(Revelation 21–22). The city will also have no need for luminary
lights in the sky. The apostle John wrote: "The city does not need
the sun or the moon to shine on it, because the glory of God
illuminates it, and its lamp is the Lamb. The nations will walk
by its light, and the kings of the earth will bring their glory into
it. Its gates will never close by day because it will never be night
there" (Rev 21:23–25). The light illuminating the new Jerusalem
will be the glorious radiant presence of God the Father and his
beloved son, Jesus Christ. No wonder the lights of Christmas
mean so much to so many.

CHAPTER 2

THE GENEALOGY OF JESUS CHRIST

MATTHEW 1:1–17

> "An account of the genealogy of Jesus Christ, the
> Son of David, the Son of Abraham."
> —Matthew 1:1

You can discover a lot about your family background today through internet searches. Sometimes what people discover is quite surprising. We may find both famous and infamous characters lurking in our family history. As we examine Jesus's family tree, we discover the same realities.

A New Beginning (1:1)

The opening line of the New Testament canon echoes the language of the first book of the Bible, Genesis ("In the beginning"). The word translated "genealogy" is the Greek word *genesis*, which can be translated as "origin" or "beginning." The arrival of Jesus the Messiah was a new beginning for humanity.

In Jesus's genealogy, we encounter forty-six people spanning approximately two thousand years. Matthew's structure of the genealogy counts fourteen generations from each major period of Jewish history (v. 17). Obviously, the names listed are selective not exhaustive, since there would be more than fourteen generations in each period. The word translated "fathered" (*gennaō*) can also mean "was the ancestor of" or "progenitor of."[1] Matthew used the practice of *gematria* to communicate the theological message of the genealogy. Gematria was the Jewish practice of ascribing numeric value to the consonants in a word.[2] David's name in Hebrew (D + V + D = 4 + 6 + 4) adds up to fourteen. In addition, David's name is the fourteenth name in the list. When you consider that Jesus is identified as the "son of David" before his identification as the "son of Abraham" in the opening verse, Matthew's intention to demonstrate Jesus's legal claim to the Davidic throne is clear. Jesus is the long-awaited Jewish Messiah.

We will not comment on each of the forty-six names, but we will highlight some of the more important names and references in the genealogy. As we proceed through the list of names, you will be surprised to see the makeup of Jesus's family tree. For example, the list includes both Jews and Gentiles: heroic figures like Abraham, Ruth, and David; immoral people like Jacob, Tamar, and Rahab; wicked people like Manasseh and Abijah; and rather nondescript individuals like Hezron and Nahshon. Jesus's family tree may not be that different from yours and mine!

---

[1] D. A. Carson, "Matthew," in *Matthew and Mark*, ed. Tremper Longman III and David E. Garland, rev. ed., vol. 9 of *The Expositor's Bible Commentary* (Grand Rapids: Zondervan, 2010), 91.

[2] Grant R. Osborne, *Matthew*, Zondervan Exegetical Commentary on the New Testament (Grand Rapids: Zondervan, 2010), 61.

This list reveals that human sin and depravity cannot stop God's providential plans.

The opening words of Matthew's Gospel carry important significance for a Judeo-Christian audience. However, as the genealogy unfolds, the truth that the gospel was written for all people, both Jews and Gentiles, is clear. Jesus (*Iēsous*) was a rather common first-century name for Jewish men. The name Jesus means "Yahweh saves." Christ (*Christos*) is used here as a title and not a name. Both Christ and Messiah mean "Anointed One."[3] Matthew's opening verse stands as both an introduction to the genealogy and to Matthew's Birth and Infancy narrative.[4]

From Abraham to David (1:2–6a)

The first section of the genealogy begins with Abraham (the father of the Jewish people) and concludes with David (Israel's greatest king).

Abraham, a Father of Many Nations

God made significant promises to Abraham:

> The LORD said to Abram: Go from your land, your relatives, and your father's house to the land that I will show you. I will make you into a great nation, I will bless you, I will make your name great, and you will be a blessing.

---

[3] On messianic expectations in Jesus's day see Craig A. Evans, "Messianism" in *Dictionary of New Testament Background*, IVP Bible Dictionary Series (Downers Grove: IVP Academic, 2000), 698–707.

[4] Craig L. Blomberg, *Matthew*, vol. 22 of *The New American Commentary* (Nashville: B&H, 1992), 52.

I will bless those who bless you, I will curse anyone who treats you with contempt, and all the peoples on earth will be blessed through you. (Gen 12:1–3)

"I will confirm my covenant that is between me and you and your future offspring throughout their generations. It is a permanent covenant to be your God and the God of your offspring after you." (Gen 17:7)

"And all the nations of the earth will be blessed by your offspring because you have obeyed my command." (Gen 22:18)

Jesus is the fulfillment of the Abrahamic promise that through Abraham's offspring all the nations of the earth will be blessed (cf. Matt 28:18–20).[5]

Judah, the Lineage of David

Abraham was the father of Isaac, and Isaac was the father of Jacob. Abraham, Isaac, and Jacob are often mentioned together as the patriarchs of Israel.[6] Jacob's twelve sons became the twelve tribes of Israel (see Gen 49:1–28). Since Matthew is tracing Jesus's *royal* ancestry, he mentions only Jacob's son, Judah. When Jacob blessed his sons, a special blessing was given to Judah: "The scepter will not depart from Judah or the staff from between his feet until he whose right it is comes and the obedience of the peoples belongs to him" (Gen 49:10).

---

[5] See Trent Hunter and Stephen J. Wellum, *Christ from Beginning to End: How the Full Story of Scripture Reveals the Full Glory of Christ* (Grand Rapids: Zondervan, 2018), 112–27.

[6] For example, see Gen 50:24; Exod 3:16; 33:1; Num 32:11; Deut 1:8.

The Book of Judges begins with anticipation mounting for a ruling individual from the line of Judah who might take Joshua's mantle like Joshua took Moses's (Judg 1:1–2; cf. Josh 1:1).[7] We might expect this individual to be Caleb or Othniel, given their early success (Judg 1:11–15). Alas, after the progression from Judah to Dan in 1:1–34, which is repeated in the judges themselves (from Othniel of Judah to Samson of Dan [3:7–16:31]), the book of Judges ends where it began—when Judah goes up, the Lord grants victory (20:48).[8] The book of Ruth, set in the period of the judges (Ruth 1:1), bridges this anticipation to the arrival of David (4:17–22), who surprisingly comes through a son from Judah's sexual immorality with Tamar (4:12, 18).

Returning to Matthew, Judah's twin sons, "Perez and Zerah," were born by Tamar (Matt 1:3; Gen 38:27–30). One might think that Judah's sin with Tamar would have disqualified him from a place in Jesus's genealogical line. Oddly enough, the psalmist wrote, "He [the Lord] rejected the tent of Joseph and did not choose the tribe of Ephraim. He chose instead the tribe of Judah, Mount Zion, which he loved" (Ps 78:67–68). Indeed, in Revelation, John identified the risen and exalted Jesus as "the Lion from the tribe of Judah" (Rev 5:5). Clearly, God's ways are not our ways (Isa 55:7–9). Jesus had a strange family tree, indeed.

In addition to the inclusion of Judah, the reference to Tamar is quite surprising for several reasons. First, typically women were

---

[7] As noted by Barry G. Webb, *The Book of Judges*, The New International Commentary on the Old Testament (Grand Rapids: Eerdmans, 2012), 95–96.

[8] Webb, *The Book of Judges*, 54.

not mentioned in Jewish genealogies. Tamar is the first of five women mentioned. The others are Rahab (v. 5a), Ruth (v. 5b), Bathsheba ("the wife of Uriah," v. 8), and Mary (v. 16). A second reason the reference to Tamar is unusual is that she was likely a Gentile, along with Rahab and Ruth, and possibly Bathsheba as well (since she was married to a Hittite). Third, Tamar and Judah, her father-in-law, engaged in sexual sin, resulting in her pregnancy. Genesis 38 provides the sordid details of how Judah had sexual relations with his daughter-in-law, whom he thought to be a Canaanite prostitute. As we will soon see, Judah and Tamar are not the only names in the genealogical list who committed acts of sexual immorality.

We do not know much about Hezron and Aram (Matt 1:3). Hezron was one of those who journeyed to Egypt with Jacob (Gen 46:12; 1 Chr 2:5). Aram (also called Ram) is mentioned in 1 Chr 2:9–15 and Ruth 4:18–19. The selective nature of the list can be seen in the fact that from Perez to Amminadab, just a few names are mentioned over a period of approximately four hundred years.[9] Similarly, not much is known of Amminadab, Nahshon, and Salmon (1:4). Amminadab and Nahshon are referenced in Exod 6:23 and Salmon in Ruth 4:18–22. Nahshon was chief of the tribe of Judah in the wilderness (Num 2:3; 10:14).

Rahab, an Unlikely Great-Grandma

The next name deserving comment is Rahab (Matt 1:5). Rahab was a prostitute who hid the Jewish spies in Jericho (Joshua 2). She became a follower of God as demonstrated by her dramatic

---

[9] Michael J. Wilkins, *Matthew: From Biblical Text to Contemporary Life*, NIV Application Commentary (Grand Rapids: Zondervan, 2004), 59.

confession of faith in the book of Joshua: "When we heard of it, our hearts melted in fear and everyone's courage failed because of you, for the LORD your God is God in heaven above and on the earth below. Now then, please swear to me by the LORD that you will show kindness to my family, because I have shown kindness to you. Give me a sure sign" (2:11–12 NIV).

The author of Hebrews names Rahab in the famous Hall of Faith (Heb 11:31). James used her as an example of the relationship between faith and good works (Jas 2:25). While Rahab had once been a terrible sinner, she believed in God's power, risked her life to hide the spies, and willingly became a part of the people of God (Heb 11:31). Rahab was justified by faith and escaped God's judgment on Jericho. One of Rahab's descendants was Boaz, the husband of Ruth. In what sense was Rahab "the mother of Boaz," since she lived approximately two hundred years earlier? We should understand the phrase "mother of" as we do "father of" in the genealogy, suggesting she was an ancestress of Boaz.[10]

Boaz was a wealthy landowner who married Ruth and rescued her from destitution and became her kinsman redeemer (Ruth 4). While no moral flaws should be attributed to Ruth's character from Scripture, that she was a Gentile, a Moabitess, is notable. The son of Boaz and Ruth was Obed (Ruth 4:13–17), who became the father of Jesse (Ruth 4:21–22), who became the father of David (v. 6). David was the youngest of Jesse's eight sons (1 Samuel 16). Matthew reminded his readers of the glorious reign and messianic promises associated with David by including the title *king* with his name.[11]

---

[10] Osborne, *Matthew*, 64; Wilkins, *Matthew*, 64.

[11] See Hunter and Wellum, *Christ from Beginning to End*, 152–68. For a study highlighting the pattern of kingship in the Bible and where

From David to Exile (1:6b–11)

The second section of the genealogy repeats the name of David
and extends to the exile (586 BC).

Solomon, a New David?

Solomon was the second child born to David and Bathsheba,
after the death of their firstborn (2 Sam 11:27–12:23). Bathsheba
is referred to simply as "Uriah's wife" (v. 6b). Bathsheba's designation as "Uriah's wife" recalls David's adulterous relationship with
her, culminating in the death of Uriah (2 Samuel 11). Solomon
was the last king of the united monarchy. While Solomon was
celebrated for his wisdom, his downfall was his thirst for luxury
and sexual promiscuity (see 1 Kgs 1–11; 2 Chr 1–9). Indeed, the
Chronicler calls attention to Solomon's acquisition of chariots
and horses, his hording of silver and gold, and the economic
return to Egypt—all of which suggest that he isn't the king the
Lord said his people needed (2 Chr 1:14–17; cf. Deut 17:16–17).

Like or Unlike David, a Royal Lineage

The remainder of this section of the genealogy consists of a striking alternation of wicked and godly kings who ruled the southern kingdom of Judah. Often, David is held up as the standard
of a godly king (e.g., 1 Kgs 14:8), fueling anticipation for a new

---

David fits into the pattern pointing to Christ see James M. Hamilton,
*Typology—Understanding the Bible's Promise-Shaped Patterns: How Old
Testament Expectations Are Fulfilled in Christ* (Grand Rapids: Zondervan,
2022), 147–73.

David. Solomon's son, Rehoboam, was not like David but was responsible for dividing the nation (Matt 1:7; 1 Kgs 12:1–24). Rehoboam fell into the trap of his father with a desire for luxury and extramarital relationships. He taxed the people heavily to support his lavish lifestyle, including his eighteen wives and sixty concubines (2 Chr 11:18–23). After the division of the kingdom, he ruled the southern kingdom called Judah, and wicked Jeroboam ruled the northern kingdom known as Israel. The focus of the genealogical names is only on the southern kingdom since Matthew's purpose is to trace the *Davidic* line to Jesus.

Abijah (also called Abijam) followed in the wicked footsteps of Rehoboam (v. 7). First Kings 15:3 captures the essence of his reign, "Abijam walked in all the sins his father before him had committed, and he was not wholeheartedly devoted to the LORD his God as his ancestor David had been." Asa, unlike his father Abijah, "did what was right in the LORD's sight, as his ancestor David had done" (1 Kgs 15:11). This will be the first example of a wicked king's son serving God faithfully, unlike his father. Asa removed pagan altars and destroyed the high places (2 Chr 14–15).

Asa was followed by his son Jehoshaphat, who also walked with God (v. 8; 1 Kgs 22:43). Jehoshaphat strengthened the reforms of his father and even impacted surrounding nations (2 Chr 17:19–20). Jehoshaphat, however, made a monumental mistake by aligning himself with wicked Ahab, the king of the northern kingdom. Jehoshaphat arranged the marriage of his son, Joram (also called Jehoram), to Ahab and Jezebel's daughter. Consequently, Joram departed from Jehoshaphat's godly example, and Joram "walked in the ways of the kings of Israel, as the house of Ahab had done, for Ahab's daughter was his wife. He did what was evil in the LORD's sight" (2 Kgs 8:18). Despite the wickedness of Joram's reign, "For the sake of his servant David, the LORD was unwilling to destroy Judah, since he had promised to give a lamp to David and his sons forever" (2 Kgs 8:19).

Matthew omits the names of the next three kings (all were wicked), likely to stay with his pattern of fourteen names. So "Joram fathered Uzziah" in the sense that Uzziah (also called Azariah) was a descendant of Joram (v. 8). Uzziah faithfully walked with God during most of his reign, but he sinned against God by becoming proud and entering the temple to burn incense, a task reserved only for the priests (2 Chr 26:16). God punished Uzziah by inflicting him with leprosy until his death. Jotham learned from his father's prideful downfall and "did not waver in obeying the LORD his God" (2 Chr 27:6). Jotham, however, did not remove the high places (2 Kgs 15:34–35). Jotham's son, Ahaz, ruled for sixteen years and "did not do what was right in the sight of the LORD his God like his ancestor David "(2 Kgs 16:2). Ahaz is described as sacrificing one of his sons in a burnt offering. In addition, he offered sacrifices and burned incense on the high places (2 Kgs 16:3–4).

Amazingly, Ahaz had a godly son, Hezekiah. Second Kings 18:5–7 summarizes his reign with the words, "Hezekiah relied on the LORD God of Israel; not one of the kings of Judah was like him, either before him or after him. He remained faithful to the LORD and did not turn from following him but kept the commands the LORD had commanded Moses. The LORD was with him, and wherever he went he prospered." When God informed Hezekiah that he was going to die, Hezekiah prayed to God, and God granted him another fifteen years of life.

Despite Hezekiah's godly reign, his son, Manasseh, may have been Judah's most wicked king. Second Chronicles 33:9 describes him this way, "So Manasseh caused Judah and the inhabitants of

Jerusalem to stray so that they did worse evil than the nations the LORD had destroyed before the Israelites." Manasseh rebuilt the high places, restored pagan altars, and sacrificed his own son. In a shocking turn of events, Manasseh later repented and turned to the Lord (2 Chr 33:13).

Manasseh's son Amon had been influenced greatly by his father's wickedness. Amon returned the nation to idol worship. His reign is summarized in 2 Chr 33:22–23: "He did what was evil in the LORD's sight, just as his father Manasseh had done. Amon sacrificed to all the carved images that his father Manasseh had made, and he served them. But he did not humble himself before the LORD like his father Manasseh humbled himself; instead, Amon increased his guilt."

In another extraordinary turn of events, wicked Amon was followed by his godly son, Josiah, who sought to undo all the wickedness of his father. Second Kings 23:25 summarizes the godly reign of Josiah: "Before him there was no king like him who turned to the LORD with all his heart and with all his soul and with all his strength according to all the law of Moses, and no one like him arose after him." Some of Josiah's most important accomplishments were the restoration of the temple, the discovery of the book of the law in the temple, and the renewal of the Passover celebration. This portion of the genealogy concludes with Josiah's grandson, Jeconiah (also called Jehoiachin; v. 11).

Jeconiah's reign was preceded by Josiah's two sons—Jehoahaz (a three-month reign) and Jehoiakim (a twelve-month reign). Neither of these is mentioned in Matthew's genealogy. This section of the genealogy concludes with Jeconiah being taken into Babylonian captivity. A section that began with a second reference to David, Israel's greatest king, concludes with one of Israel's darkest moments, Babylonian captivity.

From the Exile to the Messiah (1:12–17)

The final section of the genealogy begins with another reference to the exile and concludes with "Jesus who is called the Messiah" (v. 16).

End of the Genealogy

"Jeconiah fathered Shealtiel" (v. 12; 1 Chr 3:17), "who was the father of Zerubbabel" (v. 12; Ezra 3:2, 8). While we do not know anything more about Shealtiel, Zerubbabel himself plays a key role in Jewish history. He led a group of exiles to return to Jerusalem and began the rebuilding of the temple (Hag 2:1–5; Ezra 5:2). Haggai 2:23 records God's evaluation of Zerubbabel in these words, "'On that day'—this is the declaration of the LORD of Armies—'I will take you, Zerubbabel son of Shealtiel, my servant'—this is the LORD's declaration—'and make you like my signet ring, for I have chosen you.' This is the declaration of the LORD of Armies." After Zerubbabel, nothing is known about the other names in vv. 13–15. The probable reason for this is that they lived during the time between the Old and New Testaments.

When the genealogy finally arrives at Joseph, Matthew is clear that Joseph was not Jesus's biological father (v. 16). Matthew used the feminine relative pronoun ("from *whom*") indicating Jesus came biologically through Mary, apart from Joseph. Matthew made this even clearer when he wrote later concerning Mary's virginal conception (v. 18). As mentioned earlier, Matthew breaks Israel's history down into three periods of fourteen generations (v. 17). However, it does not appear that there are fourteen generations in each period. We likely should understand Matthew to count inclusively at times and to count exclusively at other times. For example, David's name concludes the first section of the genealogy and begins the second section as well, so David's name is counted twice.

What about Luke's Genealogy?

The relationship between Matthew's and Luke's presentations of Jesus's genealogy has provoked a significant amount of discussion.[12] Matthew's Gospel begins with Jesus's genealogy, while Luke's Gospel waits until chapter three. Matthew begins with Abraham and moves forward to Jesus. Luke, on the other hand, begins with Jesus and goes all the way back to Adam. As mentioned earlier, Matthew's genealogy is intended to prove Jesus's Davidic lineage. Luke, however, was writing primarily to a Gentile audience and wanted to connect Jesus to the Gentile Adam, suggesting Jesus is the Savior of all people. Also, by placing Adam's name just before the account of Jesus's wilderness temptation, Luke alerts his readers to the contrast between Adam's fall into temptation in the garden and Jesus's resistance of temptation in the wilderness.

A more difficult discussion is the variation between the two genealogies, especially the names between David and Jesus. When compared side by side, the differences are striking. Evangelical scholars usually follow one of two explanations.[13] The first understands Matthew's genealogy to follow Jesus's

---

[12] The complexity of the issues and possible explanations are laid out well by Darrell L. Bock, *Luke*, 2 vols., *Baker Exegetical Commentary on the New Testament* (Grand Rapids: Baker Academic, 1994), 1:918–23.

[13] See footnote 12.

legal (royal) lineage through Joseph, while Luke traces Mary's biological line from Jesus through David and to Adam. A second approach, and to be preferred, is Carson's understanding of the role that levirate marriage (Deut 25:5–6) played at one or more points in Joseph's biological ancestry (especially the names between David and Jesus).[14]

Final Reflections

The tendency of many believers is to rush past Matthew's genealogy of Jesus and begin a serious study of Christ's coming in the following passage. The names in the genealogy are hard to pronounce and most of the names seem insignificant to the first Christmas. This cannot be further from the truth. Not only is Jesus's genealogy very important, but the truths learned are very significant.

First, we learn that God can be trusted to keep his promises. Jesus's genealogy begins with Abraham, the father of the Jewish people. Abraham is a monumental figure in the Old Testament, being the first of the three great patriarchs—Abraham, Isaac, and Jacob. God *promised* Abraham a land and a seed, but even more than that, God promised Abraham that through his seed he would be a blessing to the nations. Jesus is the seed of Abraham. Because we are united to Christ through faith, we are descendants of Abraham, the father of all who believe (Gal 3:16, 29; Rom 4:16).

Second, we learn that Jesus is the Son of David. A major purpose of the genealogy is to affirm Jesus's Davidic lineage.

---

[14] Carson, "Matthew," 89–90.

Jesus is Israel's long anticipated Messiah-King. As we have seen, the structure of the genealogy focuses attention directly on David. The numerical value of David's name in Hebrew is fourteen. The genealogy is divided into three groups of fourteen names. The fourteenth name in the list is David's name. David's name is mentioned in vv. 1, 6, and 17. In the next passage, Joseph will be identified as a "son of David." The remainder of Matthew's Gospel helps his readers understand the kind of Davidic King that Jesus will be. All the hopes, dreams, and promises of the Old Testament are coming to fruition in Jesus Christ, who came not "to abolish but to fulfill" (Matt 5:17). Jesus is the divine King who will bring his people out of exile.

A third truth highlighted in Jesus's genealogy is that Jesus came for all people—Jew and Gentile, moral and immoral, the seemingly significant and the seemingly insignificant. Jesus's kingdom will encompass so many more people than most of us ever imagined. You may think your family background disqualifies you from kingdom service—think again. You may think your life before you met Jesus will keep you from being able to make a kingdom impact—think again. Some of the most wicked people in the list had godly offspring, and some who committed terrible sins found God's forgiveness and became important figures in carrying out God's will.

A Christmas Hymn of Response

What Child is this, who, laid to rest
On Mary's lap is sleeping?
Whom angels greet with anthems sweet,
While shepherds watch are keeping?
(Refrain)

Why lies He in such mean estate,
Where ox and ass are feeding?
Good Christian, fear: for sinners here
The silent Word is pleading.
(Refrain)

So bring Him incense, gold, and myrrh,
Come, peasant, king, to own Him;
The King of kings salvation brings;
Let loving hearts enthrone Him.
(Refrain)

This, this is Christ, the King,
Whom shepherds guard and angels sing:
Haste, haste to bring Him laud,
The Babe, the Son of Mary![15]

Taking a Deeper Dive: The Son of David

Matthew, more than any other Gospel writer, emphasizes Jesus as the Son of David. Many first-century Jews believed the Davidic Messiah would be a warrior throwing off the yoke of Roman domination and restoring Israel's kingdom.[16] David was clearly Israel's greatest king. God made a promise to David that he would always have a descendant to reign over the house of Israel and God would be his Father. The most important of these promises is 2 Sam 7:12–16, which reads,

---

[15] William Dix, "What Child Is This?" 1865, *Baptist Hymnal*, #118.
[16] See Mark L. Strauss, *Luke*, Zondervan Illustrated Bible Backgrounds Commentary (Grand Rapids: Zondervan, 2002), 17.

"When your time comes and you rest with your ancestors, I will raise up after you your descendant, who will come from your body, and I will establish his kingdom. He is the one who will build a house for my name, and I will establish the throne of his kingdom forever. I will be his father, and he will be my son. When he does wrong, I will discipline him with a rod of men and blows from mortals. But my faithful love will never leave him as it did when I removed it from Saul, whom I removed from before you. Your house and kingdom will endure before me forever, and your throne will be established forever."

God's promise of a Davidic descendant on the throne seemed doomed with the destruction of Jerusalem and the Babylonian exile. Despite this dire situation, both the royal psalms (e.g., Psalms 89; 132) and prophets (e.g., Isa 11:1; Jer 33:17–22) encouraged God's people to hold out hope for a coming Davidic Messiah. During the time between the testaments, the hopes for a restored Davidic kingdom resulted in a renewed longing for a coming Messiah from David's line.[17]

Matthew uses the title "Son of David" for Jesus nine times (see Matt 1:1; 9:27; 12:23; 15:22; 20:30, 31; 21:9, 15; 22:42).[18] Mark uses the title three times (10:47, 48, 12:35), and Luke uses the title five times (1:32; 3:31; 18:38, 39; 20:41). Although John never uses the title "Son of David," he does refer to Jesus as "David's offspring" once (John 7:42).

---

[17] For a survey of Old Testament and intertestamental Messianic scholarship, see Stanley E. Porter, *The Messiah in the Old and New Testaments* (Grand Rapids: Eerdmans, 2007), 4–6.

[18] In several of Matthew's passages, those who address Jesus as the "Son of David" are the disenfranchised.

The Christological importance of Jesus's Davidic lineage is emphasized in Matthew's Birth and Infancy narrative in both the genealogy (1:1–17) and the visit of the magi, who are searching for the "King of the Jews" (2:1–12). At Jesus's triumphal entry into Jerusalem on Palm Sunday, many in the crowd acknowledged Jesus to be the Son of David (21:1–11). The significance of the moment is caught in the crowd's cry of Ps 118:25–26: "*Hosanna* to the Son of David! Blessed is he who comes in the name of the Lord! *Hosanna* in the highest heaven!" (21:9). The last use of the phrase "Son of David" in Matthew is in an exchange between Jesus and the Pharisees. "Jesus asked them, 'What do you think about the Messiah? Whose son is he?' 'The son of David,' they replied. He said to them, 'How is it then that David, speaking by the Spirit, calls him 'Lord'?" (22:41–43 NIV). Jesus then quotes Psalm 110. Although Jesus is David's Son, he is also David's Lord and God. Clearly, the first Christmas is in part about the fulfilment of God's promise to David that one day a descendant of his would sit on his throne and his kingdom would never end.

CHAPTER 3

THE ANNUNCIATION OF THE FORERUNNER

LUKE 1:5–25

> "Do not be afraid, Zechariah, because your prayer
> has been heard. Your wife Elizabeth will bear you
> a son, and you will name him John."
> —Luke 1:13

After four hundred years of divine silence, God broke his silence by speaking through an angel to an elderly priest serving in the Jerusalem temple. Luke's Birth and Infancy narrative is structured around an alternating focus on John the Baptist and Jesus. The Gospel of Luke begins with the annunciation (announcement) of John's birth to Zechariah (1:5–25) and then the annunciation of Jesus's birth to Mary (1:26–38). Next, Luke describes the meeting of Mary and Elizabeth (1:39–56). Luke then recounts the birth, circumcision, and naming of John (1:57–80). Finally, Luke retells the birth, circumcision, and naming of Jesus, along with a key moment at the temple when Jesus was twelve years old (2:1–52).

At every turn, Jesus is depicted as greater than John.[1] While John's conception is miraculous, it was the result of the sexual union between the elderly Zechariah and Elizabeth. Jesus was conceived by a virgin. While John would be the prophet of the Most High, Jesus was the Son of the Most High. While John would be a prophet, Jesus was the Messiah. While John was truly great, Jesus was incomparably greater.

A Heartbreaking Situation: Childlessness (1:5–7)

The story begins during the reign of Herod the Great.[2] The Roman senate granted Herod the title "king of the Jews" in 40 BC. Herod, however, did not solidify his rule until 37 BC and then ruled over the Jewish people until his death in 4 BC. Herod's rule was a dark time for God's people. His reign was characterized by brutality and paranoia, yet no one could have anticipated what God was doing during those horrendous years.

Zechariah, an elderly priest, is the next name to appear in the narrative, after Herod (v. 5). The differences between Herod and Zechariah could not be greater. While Herod ruled as a brutal dictator, Zechariah was a faithful follower of God. While Herod was involved in the expansion and beautification of the temple for his own glory, Zechariah served God in the temple

---

[1] Walter L. Liefeld and David W. Pao, "Luke," in *Luke–Acts*, ed. Tremper Longman III and David E. Garland, The Expositor's Bible Commentary (Grand Rapids: Zondervan, 2007), 52.

[2] For a recent discussion on Herod the Great see Helen Bond, "Herodian Dynasty," in *Dictionary of Jesus and the Gospels*, ed. Joel B. Green, 2nd ed. (Downers Grove: IVP Academic, 2013), 379–82.

as a faithful priest for God's glory. While Herod would attempt to kill the baby Jesus, Zechariah was the father of the forerunner of Jesus.

Zechariah ("God remembers") served in the priestly division of Abijah. Abijah was one of the heads of the priestly families mentioned in 1 Chr 24:7–18 (cf. Neh 12:1–7). Twenty-four divisions of priests served two one-week periods annually in the temple.[3] During the major festivals, as many priests as were able would travel to Jerusalem to serve.

Luke informs his readers concerning three matters about Zechariah and his wife, Elizabeth (vv. 5–7). First, both Zechariah and Elizabeth were from a priestly lineage. While a priest was not required to marry a woman of priestly ancestry, Zechariah's marriage to Elizabeth further demonstrates his godliness. Second, they were both "righteous [*dikaios*] in God's sight, living without blame [*amemptos*] according to all the commands and requirements of the Lord" (v. 6). For Luke to indicate they were righteous "in God's sight" means that their godliness was genuine and not hypocritical. To state the matter another way, their public and private lives corresponded. While they were not perfect, their home was filled with loving devotion to God. Third, they were childless. Luke's description of the elderly couple's godliness was to help his readers understand that their childlessness was not God's punishment.[4]

Elizabeth's barrenness would have resulted in both great cultural shame and personal anguish (1 Sam 1:5–6; 2 Sam 6:23; Jer 22:30). Psalm 127:3–5 catches something of the deep grief the

---

[3] Mark L. Strauss, *Luke*, Zondervan Illustrated Bible Backgrounds Commentary (Grand Rapids: Zondervan, 2022), 10.

[4] Liefeld and Pao, "Luke," 54.

couple must have experienced: "Behold, children are a heritage
from the LORD, the fruit of the womb a reward. Like arrows in
the hand of a warrior are the children of one's youth. Blessed
is the man who fills his quiver with them! He shall not be put
to shame when he speaks with his enemies in the gate" (ESV).
The fact that Zechariah and Elizabeth were elderly indicates
they were past childbearing years and Elizabeth's conception
of John would be miraculous. For the sensitive reader, the mention of a godly couple without children would recall several Old
Testament couples in a similar situation.

- Abraham and Sarah (Gen 11:30; 21:1–7)
- Isaac and Rebekah (Gen 25:21–24)
- Jacob and Rachel (Gen 29:31–30:20; 35:11–17)
- Manoah and his wife (Judg 13:1–25)
- Elkanah and Hannah (1 Sam 1:1–20)

A Providential Moment (1:8–10)

Little did Zechariah know how dramatically his life would
change on the day he was chosen by lot to serve in the temple. The casting of lots is comparable to throwing dice.[5] Prior
to the coming of the Holy Spirit at Pentecost, casting lots was
an accepted method for discerning God's will. Proverbs 16:33
states, "The lot is cast into the lap, but its every decision is from
the LORD."[6]

---

[5] Strauss, *Luke*, 10.

[6] The following are examples of the casting of lots in the Old
Testament: determining God's will (Num 27:21), dividing up allot-
ments in the Promised Land (Josh 18:11), allocating military tasks (Judg
20:9–10), appointing families to resettle in Jerusalem (Neh 11:1), assigning

The task assigned to Zechariah that day was to burn incense in the Holy Place (Exod 30:7–8).[7] Zechariah would have walked through the Court of the Gentiles, the Court of the Women, the Court of the Priests, and then entered the Holy Place. This would be Zechariah's only opportunity to perform that sacred task.[8] The lot falling to him demonstrates God's providence in his selection on that day. Each day, once in the morning and again in the evening, a priest offered fresh incense to be burned on the altar of incense in the Holy Place. When Luke referred to the Holy Place, or the Most Holy Place, he used the term *naos,* but when he referred to the larger temple complex, he used the word *hieron.* The High Priest alone entered the Most Holy Place once a year on the Day of Atonement (Leviticus 16). Along with the altar of incense, the Holy Place contained the table of showbread and the golden lampstand (Exod 30:1–10; 37:25–29).

At the same time as the burning of the incense, animal sacrifices took place on the great altar in the temple courtyard. When the people saw the smoke from the burning incense, they would pray. The smoke rising toward heaven symbolized the people's prayers ascending to God. After the priest offered the incense, he exited the Holy Place and pronounced a blessing on the

---

responsibilities to Levites and priests (1 Chr 24:5–18), and settling disputes (Prov 18:18). The final time we read about the casting of lots is the selection of Matthias as a replacement for Judas (Acts 1:26).

[7] For a discussion on the Tamid Service see David E. Garland, *Luke,* Zondervan Exegetical Commentary on the New Testament (Grand Rapids: Zondervan, 2012), 64–65.

[8] I. H. Marshall, *The Gospel of Luke,* The New International Greek Testament Commentary (Grand Rapids: Eerdmans, 1978), 54; Strauss, *Luke,* 11.

gathered worshipers. David Garland describes what would have taken place.

> In the afternoon sacrifice, the incense was last, and the assigned priest and two assistants carried burning coals from the great altar into the chamber of the Holy Place to burn the incense on the altar of incense, made of gold-plated wood and located in the center of the room before the veil separating the Holy Place from the Most Holy Place (Exod 30:1–10). The assistants then withdrew, leaving the priest alone in the sanctuary, when he would lay the incense on the coals at the signal of the presiding priest and prostrate himself in prayer.[9]

An Angelic Announcement (1:11–17)

Zechariah was completely unprepared for what he experienced that day. His heart would have been filled with joy because he was entering the Holy Place. Zechariah no sooner entered than he encountered the angel, Gabriel.

The Angel's Appearance (1:11–12)

The angelic appearance and announcement follow a pattern found in other Old Testament birth announcements (Gen 16:7–13; 17:1–21; 18:1–15). Luke identifies the angel as "an angel of the Lord." Only later does Gabriel identify himself to Zechariah (v. 19). Gabriel's appearance was burned into Zechariah's memory as he recounted later the exact location where Gabriel stood

---

[9] Garland, *Luke*, 64.

("on the right side of the altar of incense"). Approximately five hundred years earlier, Gabriel had appeared to Daniel in Babylon (Dan 8:16). Zechariah was overcome by fear, as Daniel had been (Dan 8:17). After calming Zechariah's fear, Gabriel encouraged Zechariah with the news that his prayer had been heard. We do not know to what specific prayer Gabriel refers. Zechariah may have been praying for the coming of the Messiah as he performed his sacred tasks. If so, the prayer for a coming Messiah would be fulfilled soon. Or more likely, Gabriel referred to Zechariah's prayer for a child, since Gabriel went on to indicate Elizabeth would give birth to a son. One would presume the couple had ceased praying for a child long ago, since Elizabeth was well beyond childbearing years and Zechariah expressed doubt about the possibility of his wife conceiving a child. After years of great disappointment, their prayers for a child were soon to be answered.[10] Although there was a long delay between their initial request for a child and God's answer, the delay was worth the wait. Zechariah soon discovered his son would be the forerunner of the Messiah.[11]

Angels (*angelos*) play an important role in both Matthew's and Luke's Birth and Infancy narratives and have an equally important role in the Resurrection narratives. Much of what people believe about angels comes from Christmas ornaments,

---

[10] Prayer plays an important role in Luke's Gospel. Luke describes Jesus praying at every key moment in his ministry (3:21; 5:16; 6:12; 9:18, 29; 10:21; 11:1; 22:31–32, 40, 46; 23:4, 43).

[11] The psalms have many verses on God hearing/answering his people's prayers. The following are a brief sample: 6:8–9; 18:6; 28:6; 31:22; 34:17; 145:19.

paintings, and television programs. Angels are spirit-beings created by God to serve his purposes and are found throughout the Scriptures. Angels are called by a variety of names including *seraphim*, *cherubim*, and *living creatures*. Sometimes angels manifest themselves as men and at times are described as wearing shining garments (Matt 28:3; Mark 16:5). Angelic beings can be found in the Scriptures guarding the entrance to Eden, waging war in the heavenlies, rescuing Peter from prison, worshiping in the presence of God, and delivering messages from God (Gen 3:24; Dan 10:10–21; Matt 1:13–17; Acts 11:6–10; Revelation 4–5). Only two angels are named specifically in the Bible, Michael ("Who is like God?") and Gabriel ("Warrior/Hero of God").[12]

Gabriel's Good News (1:13–17)

Gabriel provided details to Zechariah of several key features related to John's birth and subsequent ministry (vv. 13–17). First, his name was to be *John* ("the Lord is gracious"). In the Old Testament, when God named a child that child played an important role in God's plans.[13] Second, John's birth would result in boundless joy. Joy and rejoicing are key themes in Luke's opening chapters (1:44, 47, 58; 2:10). Nehemiah wrote, "The joy of the LORD is your strength" (Neh 8:10). Israel had been living in darkness, but the light of God's glory was beginning to dawn. Joy and strength were coming to the righteous remnant.

Third, John will be great in God's sight. John's greatness was due to his prophetic role as the forerunner of the Messiah.

---

[12] Strauss, *Luke*, 12.

[13] For other examples see Gen 16:8, 11; 17:19; 1 Kgs 13:2; Isa 7:14; 9:1; Matt 1:21; Luke 1:31.

Greatness in God's eyes is vastly different from greatness in the world's eyes. Greatness in the world's eyes is determined by income, possessions, and fame. John would live an ascetic life, suffer for his faith, and die a martyr's death. What a contrast between the Kingdom of God and the kingdoms of this world. Jesus would say later, "I tell you, among those born of women no one is greater than John" (Luke 7:28).

Fourth, the fact that "John will never drink wine (*oinos*) or beer" (*sikera*) implied he would live a consecrated life (v. 15). Since no mention is made of *not* cutting his hair, it is unlikely this is a Nazarite vow (Num 6:5; Judg 13:4–5). Instead, John's abstinence meant his entire life was to be set apart to fulfill God's call on his life. In John's lifelong abstinence from alcohol, he was like Samson and Samuel (Judg 13:4–7; 1 Sam 1:11, 15).[14] Both Samson and Samuel functioned as leaders of God's people during difficult days.

Fifth, the Holy Spirit would empower John's life and ministry. John would be filled with the Spirit while "still in his mother's womb" (v. 15; cf. Jer 1:5). The Holy Spirit plays a prominent role throughout Luke's Gospel, but especially in the Birth and Infancy narrative. In response to Mary's bewilderment about how she could conceive a child while still a virgin, Gabriel said to her, "The Holy Spirit will come upon you, and the power of the Most High will overshadow you" (1:35). Elizabeth was filled with the Spirit and prophesied when she encountered Mary (1:41). When John was formally named, Zechariah's tongue was loosed, he was filled with the Spirit, and he prophesied (1:67). Simeon was a member of the righteous remnant, and the Spirit was upon him (2:25–27). The Spirit led him into the temple complex at just the

---

[14] Strauss, *Luke*, 12.

right time to encounter Joseph, Mary, and the baby Jesus. Clearly, the age of the Spirit was dawning.

Sixth, John called God's people to return to covenant faithfulness. God's Spirit empowered him to preach boldly and courageously to a people whose hearts were callous and cold toward God. Gabriel alluded to the future *success* of John's ministry (italics added):

> He *will* turn many of the children of Israel to the Lord their God. And he *will* go before him in the spirit and power of Elijah, to *turn* the hearts of fathers to their children, and the disobedient to the understanding of the righteous, to make ready for the Lord a prepared people. (1:16–17)

The word "turn" (*epistrephō*) is used twice in these verses and suggests a change in direction, analogous to repentance and conversion.

Seventh, John's prophetic ministry was like Elijah's prophetic ministry ("he will go before the Lord in the spirit and power of Elijah") (Mal 3:1; 4:6; cf. Isa 40:3–5). Gabriel referred to the final verses in Malachi, emphasizing the connection between Elijah and John. Like Elijah, John's message was powerful and filled with dire warnings of coming judgment to recalcitrant Israel. John was not Elijah, however, as Jesus made clear.

- For all the prophets and the law prophesied until John. And if you're willing to accept it, he is the Elijah who is to come. (Matt 11:13–14)
- So the disciples asked him, "Why then do the scribes say that Elijah must come first?" "Elijah is coming and will restore everything," he replied. "But I tell you: Elijah has already come, and they didn't recognize him. On

the contrary, they did whatever they pleased to him. In the same way the Son of Man is going to suffer at their hands." Then the disciples understood that he had spoken to them about John the Baptist. (Matt 17:10–13)

Finally, John's ultimate purpose was to prepare people for the coming of the Lord. John accomplished his purpose so well that some thought he might be the Messiah (Luke 3:15; John 1:20). He rejected the idea and did not consider himself worthy to untie the Messiah's sandals (John 3:27–30). Gabriel's description of John's person and ministry highlighted his irreplaceable role in salvation history. David Gooding sums up the scene this way,

> Isaiah had prophesied (40:3–5) that before the "glory of the Lord" should "be revealed," a forerunner would be sent to prepare the way of the Lord. Malachi had added that before the day of the Lord came, the prophet Elijah would be sent to "turn the hearts of the fathers to the children and the hearts of the children to their fathers . . ." (4:5–6). And now more than 400 years after Malachi the seemingly interminable night was coming to its end: the dawn was about to break.[15]

Doubt, Punishment, and Fulfillment (1:18–25)

The closing verses of this section begin with Zechariah questioning Gabriel concerning Elizabeth's conception of a child and conclude with Gabriel's words coming to fruition.

---

[15] David Gooding, *According to Luke: The Third Gospel's Ordered Historical Narrative* (Belfast, NIR: Myrtlefield House, 2013), 28.

Zechariah Doubted Gabriel's Reply (1:18–20)

Zechariah informed Gabriel that he and his wife were elderly, as if Gabriel did not know. Zechariah failed to remember that, throughout the Scripture, our impossibilities are the stage on which God performs some of his greatest works. As a faithful follower of God, Zechariah knew the biblical stories of God granting children to infertile couples. Zechariah's problem was that he could not conceive of God doing for them what God had done for others. What was true of Zechariah may be equally true of us. Standing before Zechariah was an angel of God, delivering to him a message from the divine throne room. But still Zechariah questioned the possibility of Elizabeth's conceiving a child. Zechariah's failure to believe Gabriel's words brought divine chastisement. The elderly priest would remain mute (*kōphos*) and presumably deaf for nine months, unable to verbalize his encounter with Gabriel. Yet, God's graciousness was on full display in that he kept his word despite Zechariah's doubts.

Zechariah Exited the Temple Unable to Speak (1:21–23)

Those who gathered to pray wondered why Zechariah was taking so long to complete his priestly tasks (v. 21). When he emerged, he could not speak and communicated by hand gestures. The crowd understood Zechariah to have seen a vision. At the conclusion of Zechariah's service (*leitourgia*) at the temple, he returned home.

Promise Fulfilled and Shame Removed (1:24–25)

After his return, Elizabeth conceived a child, and her heart must have been filled with joy and gratitude to God for taking away the reproach of her childlessness: "The Lord has done this for me. He has looked with favor in these days to take away my disgrace among the people" (v. 25). Strangely, she remained in seclusion for five months. We are not told why she hid herself away. Possibly she wanted to make sure that she was truly pregnant. There can be little doubt that this elderly lady sang psalms of praise to God for his goodness to her.

Final Reflections

This passage has much to teach every follower of Jesus. After four hundred years of waiting, God broke his silence, not through a prophet, priest, or king, but through an angel. The message was not delivered to a prophet or a king, but to an elderly priest serving faithfully in the temple. The angel's message was spoken not only to a priest but to one who was childless. Zechariah learned very quickly from Gabriel that Elizabeth would not only have a son but that this son would be the forerunner of the Messiah. Their son would fulfill the prophecies associated with Elijah.

This promise of a son came to Zechariah and Elizabeth after a lifetime of infertility. This reality reminds us that godly people can experience great disappointments in this world. These disappointments are a reminder that we are not home yet. God has not yet wiped away every tear from our eyes. Following Jesus means that sometimes we must follow him during seasons (or decades) of disappointment. We must learn to trust God even when we don't understand his plans for us. This is the reason Zechariah and Elizabeth were an excellent choice to be the parents of John. Despite heartache and likely public ridicule over their childlessness, they had continued to walk faithfully with God. While their love for God did not remove the pain of childlessness, it demonstrated they loved God more than they loved themselves. This is a lesson all of us must learn. God is not as interested in making us happy as he is in making us holy. Obviously, this thought can be taken too far and made to mean God has no concern for our happiness and joy. Maybe another way to state the same idea is that God is more interested in our holiness than our comfort. For example, the apostle Paul experienced great suffering during his Christian life. Despite the suffering Paul experienced, he followed hard after God. Elizabeth and Zechariah demonstrate the same truth: following hard after God, despite great disappointment, brings glory to God.

By God's selection of Zechariah and Elizabeth and, later, Joseph, Mary, Simeon, and Anna, we learn God *primarily* uses godly people in the accomplishment of his plans. They were not perfect people (none of us are), but they demonstrated their love for God by their godly character. Furthermore, often the people God uses are relatively unknown, like those mentioned above. Little did they know, as they lived in relative obscurity, that God was preparing them so he could use them in his unfolding plan of redemption.

Too often we associate greatness with worldly accomplishments, large churches, and massive ministries; but sometimes the greatest among us are unknown and unseen. They may be serving Jesus in a soup kitchen in the slums of a large city. They may be a crippled lady who spends several hours a day in prayer. They may be a pastor and wife serving God faithfully in a small rural community, although there is little hope of substantial numerical growth. The people God used in preparation for Jesus's coming into the world were faithful but not necessarily successful in the world's eyes.

As we close this section, let us consider disappointment in our lives. What if the pregnancy never comes, the marriage proposal is never heard, or the dream job never materializes? We do not have to pretend that there is no disappointment or heartache, but we must recognize that God's plans may not be our plans. God's path for us may not be what we would have chosen, but we can trust him because he has demonstrated his love for us by sending his Son. When God does not part the Red Sea, does not multiply the fish and the bread, or does not perform a miracle on our behalf, do not think this means he loves you less than he loves others. Instead, trust he has a better plan and a different path for our lives. God's love is profoundly demonstrated by the sending of his Son. The first Christmas should stir in us confidence in God's commitment to all his children.

A Christmas Hymn of Response

O come, all ye faithful, joyful and triumphant,
O come ye, O come ye, to Bethlehem!
Come and behold Him,
Born the King of Angels!
O come, let us adore Him,
O come, let us adore Him,
O come, let us adore Him,
Christ the Lord!

God of God, Light of Light
Lo, He abhors not the Virgin's womb
Very God
Begotten, not created
O come, let us adore Him,

O come, let us adore Him,
O come, let us adore Him,
Christ the Lord!

Sing, choirs of angels, sing in exultation,
sing, all ye bright hosts of heav'n above!
Glory to God,
All glory in the highest!
O come, let us adore Him,
O come, let us adore Him,
O come, let us adore Him,
Christ the Lord!

Yea, Lord, we greet Thee, born this happy morning,
Jesus, to Thee be all glory giv'n;
Word of the Father,
Now in flesh appearing!
O come, let us adore Him,
O come, let us adore Him,
O come, let us adore Him,
Christ the Lord![16]

Taking a Deeper Dive: John the Baptist

Considering Gabriel's words concerning John, it may be helpful to see how those words came to pass in John's life and ministry. John's importance in the storyline of Scripture cannot be
overstated. The Synoptic Gospels describe Jesus being baptized
by John (Mark 1:9–11; Matt 3:13–17; Luke 3:21–22), and the
Fourth Gospel implies it (John 1:32–33). Mark's Gospel makes

---

[16] John Francis Wade, "O Come, All Ye Faithful," *Baptist Hymnal*, #89.

clear that Jesus waited to begin his great Galilean ministry until after John's arrest (Mark 1:14).

John prepared the way for Jesus's arrival on the scene by raising Messianic expectations in his call for national repentance. In fact, many thought John himself might be the Messiah, an idea he rejected. John, however, clearly understood himself to be the forerunner of the Messiah, seeing himself to be the fulfillment of Isa 40:3. When asked by the Jerusalem leadership to identify himself he said, "I am a voice of one crying out in the wilderness: Make straight the way of the Lord—just as Isaiah the prophet said" (John 1:23).

After John the Baptist's arrest, Jesus taught that John was more than a prophet and was the greatest human being up to that time in history (Luke 7:24–28). John's greatness was the consequence of being the forerunner of the Messiah. John's ministry had such a wide-ranging impact that Herod Antipas thought Jesus might be John come back from the dead (Mark 6:14). A final example of John's greatness is that approximately thirty years after his death, Paul encountered followers of John in the city of Ephesus (Acts 19:1–7).

Luke summarizes John's preaching in three main thoughts. First, we find a call to repentance considering the coming eschatological judgment (Luke 3:7–10). John the Baptist warned his hearers not to count on their Jewish heritage for their salvation in the coming judgment ("God is able to raise up children for Abraham from these stones," 3:8). A second aspect of John's teaching was spelling out to the crowds, tax collectors, and soldiers regarding "the fruit of repentance": sharing, honesty, and contentment (3:11–14). This simple but pointed instruction teaches us that following God manifests itself in practical daily living. No one could misunderstand the simple but powerful demonstrations of repentance spoken by John. Third, John directed the crowd's attention away from himself and towards the coming Messiah (3:15–18). As mentioned above, John rejected any thought that he was the Messiah. He felt himself unworthy even to loosen the strap from the Messiah's sandal. John did not make his ministry about himself, but about the coming Messiah. John did not demonstrate the slightest inclination of self-promotion or self-preservation. We need more men and women of God like John the Baptist serving in the church today.

Matthew's description of John's food and clothing are reminiscent of Elijah (Matt 3:4–6). By living in the desert and wearing "prophetic" style clothing and eating honey and wild locusts, John communicated his rejection of the opulence of the aristocracy in Jerusalem. His lifestyle was a visual protest of the self-indulgence of the religious establishment. Jesus made a similar point when speaking about John.

> After John's messengers left, he began to speak to the crowds about John: "What did you go out into the wilderness to see? A reed swaying in the wind? What then did you go out to see? A man dressed in soft clothes. See, those who are splendidly dressed and live in luxury are in royal palaces. What then did you go out to see? A prophet? Yes, I tell you, and more than a prophet." (Luke 7:24–26)

All of this indicates that John's lifestyle did not contradict his message but confirmed it. In our age when some preachers have become celebrities and demand treatment comparable to rock stars, John by contrast lived a life that demonstrated faithfulness to God. John's courageous preaching was on full display when he condemned Herod Antipas for taking his brother's wife

(Mark 6:16–29). John's condemnation of Antipas so infuriated Antipas's wife that with the collaboration of her daughter they put Antipas in the situation where he had to have John decapitated.

Everything Gabriel said of John was true. God used him in a phenomenal way as the forerunner of Jesus. Despite his popularity with the crowds, he never forgot he was not the Messiah but had been sent ahead of him. His final words in John's Gospel are, "He [Jesus] must increase, but I must decrease" (John 3:30). A dangerous place for a man or woman of God is to be used by God in a significant way. The temptation to slowly make ministry more about oneself than Jesus is ever too real. When asked who he was, John replied, "A voice in the wilderness," just a voice. The only way to keep yourself from falling into the sin of self-importance is to keep your eyes on Jesus. But when you do, it may cost you your life, just as it did John the Baptist.

CHAPTER 4

THE ANNUNCIATION
OF THE SON OF GOD

LUKE 1:26–38

> The Holy Spirit will come upon you,
> and the power of the Most High will
> overshadow you. Therefore, the holy one to
> be born will be called the Son of God.
> —Luke 1:35

The encounter between Gabriel and Mary stands out as one of the most dramatic moments in Scripture. Several similarities between the annunciations to Zechariah and Mary are evident. Both were visited by the angel Gabriel and were addressed by name. Both were naturally frightened by the angel's unexpected appearance and received reassurance of God's favor toward them. Both Zechariah and Mary were promised a son and told their child would be great. Each of them received instruction on what to name their child and given a sign (muteness for Zechariah and the information that Elizabeth was pregnant for Mary). Finally, the Spirit played a prominent role in both announcements.

Along with these similarities, there are significant differences between the two announcements. The first announcement was made in Jerusalem, the most important city in the Jewish religion, while the second took place in a small insignificant Galilean village, Nazareth. The first announcement was to a Jewish priest, while the second was made to a young lady. Mary was likely a young teenager.[1] The first announcement was made while Zechariah was performing his priestly duty in the temple, the heart of the Jewish faith, while the second was made to Mary as she was likely working in her parents' home. The first announcement concerned a miraculous conception by an elderly woman through the sexual relationship of a husband and wife, while the second was a miraculous conception that exceeded anything in human history, a virginal conception.

An Ordinary Setting and an Extraordinary Young Lady (1:26–27)

As mentioned above, the setting for the encounter between Gabriel and Mary was Nazareth. In John 1:46, Nathaniel asked Philip the question, "Can anything good come out of Nazareth?" Nazareth is not mentioned anywhere in the Old Testament or in any Jewish writings of the day. Joseph Fitzmyer notes that a pre-Christian mention of Nazareth was not found until 1962.[2] Nazareth was in Galilee, the region just north of Samaria and

---

[1] Raymond E. Brown, *The Birth of the Messiah: A Commentary on the Infancy Narratives in Matthew and Luke* (Garden City, NJ: Doubleday, 1981), 304. Brown indicates she may have been as young as twelve.

[2] Joseph A. Fitzmyer, *The Gospel According to Luke*, vol. 1, Anchor Bible (Garden City: Doubleday, 1981), 343.

ruled by Herod the Great's son, Herod Antipas. Nazareth is located approximately sixty-five miles north of Jerusalem and twenty miles west of the Sea of Galilee. This village was where Jesus grew from childhood into manhood. God could hardly have chosen a more obscure place for the announcement of the conception of his Son.

The Setting for the Angelic Appearance (1:26–27)

The mention of the "sixth month" ties this passage closely to the preceding passage in Luke (1:5–25).[3] Once again, God commissioned Gabriel (although he never identified himself to Mary) to deliver a message of good news to her, as he did to Zechariah. We learn two important facts about Mary (*Mariam*) in v. 27. First, Mary (meaning "excellence") was a virgin (*parthenos*), and second, she was engaged (*mnēsteuō*) to Joseph.[4] Mary's virginity will be stated again in v. 34.

Betrothal ("engagement") in ancient Judaism was a much more binding relationship than a contemporary engagement.[5] A betrothal began with a formal agreement between families that one family's son would marry another family's daughter.[6]

---

[3] See Darrell L. Bock, *Luke,* Baker Exegetical Commentary on the New Testament, 2 vols. (Grand Rapids: Baker Academic, 1994), 1:106; and David E. Garland, *Luke,* Zondervan Exegetical Commentary on the New Testament (Grand Rapids: Zondervan, 2011), 78.

[4] Bock, *Luke,* 1:107. For a lengthier discussion of Mary's descent, see Bock, *Luke,* 1:107–8.

[5] On "Jewish Marriage Customs: Betrothal and Wedding," see Michael J. Wilkins, *Matthew,* Zondervan Illustrated Bible Backgrounds Commentary (Grand Rapids: Zondervan, 2002), 11.

[6] Bock, *Luke,* 1:107.

The agreement was so binding that it could only be broken by death or divorce. In addition, there was a bride-price to be paid by the groom's family. At this point, the bride was considered the groom's wife. [7] The couple would continue to live with their parents for approximately a year without sexually consummating the marriage.[8] At the end of the process, a marriage ceremony would be held, and the couple would consummate the marriage and begin living together. Although Luke does not tell us Mary's age, the practice of a girl entering betrothal as early as twelve was not uncommon.[9] The same would be true for the groom. Neither Luke nor Matthew, however, provide the ages of Mary and Joseph. Joseph, rather than Mary, is identified as a descendant of David (v. 27).[10]

The Virgin Birth (Conception)

The virgin birth is a controversial topic in scholarly discussion.[11] The term describes the virginal conception of Mary with the child Jesus as the result of the powerful working of the Holy Spirit. Many biblical scholars reject the idea that Jesus was

---

[7] Bock, *Luke*, 1:107. See also Garland, *Luke*, 78–79.

[8] Bock, *Luke*, 1:107.

[9] Bock, *Luke*, 1:107; Mark L. Strauss, *Luke,* Zondervan Illustrated Bible Backgrounds Commentary (Grand Rapids: Zondervan, 2022), 10.

[10] Garland, *Luke*, 79.

[11] For a more complete discussion on the virgin birth, see Robert H. Stein, *Jesus the Messiah: A Survey of the Life of Christ* (Downers Grove: IVP Academic, 1996), 63–80; H. Douglas Buckwalter, "Virgin Birth" in *Evangelical Dictionary of Biblical Theology*, ed. Walter A. Elwell (Grand Rapids: Baker, 1996), 799–802. The classic work on the subject is J. Gresham Machen, *The Virgin Birth* (Grand Rapids: Baker, 1930).

conceived by a virgin. However, a belief in the reality of the virgin birth is primarily a statement about one's view of the truthfulness of Scripture. The Bible explicitly teaches Jesus's virgin birth, or more appropriately virginal conception (the birth was normal, but the conception was miraculous). Furthermore, many who reject the truthfulness of the virgin birth often deny the possibility of miracles. Christians believe if God can create the universe out of nothing (Genesis 1), then believing in the virgin birth of Jesus is reasonable. Both Luke and Matthew believed Mary to be a virgin when she conceived Jesus. Gabriel's statement to Mary that "nothing is impossible with God" encouraged her to believe in something with no historical precedent—a virginal conception (v. 37).

The present passage includes several features that portray Mary's pregnancy taking place apart from sexual intercourse with a man. First, Luke clearly describes Mary as a virgin betrothed to Joseph (v. 27). Sexual intercourse during the betrothal period was forbidden. Second, Mary's statement, "How can this be, since I have not had sexual relations with a man?" (literally "known a man") (v. 34). Third, Gabriel described Mary's conception as the result of the Holy Spirit coming over her and the power of the Most High overshadowing her (v. 35). Gabriel's point was that the conception would be a supernatural work of God. Luke intended to communicate to his readers in Jesus's genealogy that Joseph was not Jesus's biological father: "As he began his ministry, Jesus was about thirty years old and was thought to be the son of Joseph" (3:23).

While we will explore Matthew's account in more detail in chapter 7, Matthew adds several corroborating points to substantiate the historicity of Jesus's virgin birth. First, when Joseph discovered that Mary was pregnant, he intended to end their betrothal by divorce (Matt 1:18–19). Joseph knew he had not had sexual relations with her; therefore, the baby could not be his child. Second, Matthew understood the virginal conception to be the fulfillment of Isaiah 7:14 (Matt 1:22–23).[12] Third, Matt 1:25 indicates that Joseph had no sexual relations with Mary until after Jesus's birth. Thus, there would be no possibility of the child being his biological son.

While the only direct statements on the virginal conception are found in Matthew and Luke, one possible allusion is found in John 8:41. Jesus's enemies questioned him concerning his father's identity. Jesus said, "You're doing what your father does" (John 8:41). "We weren't born of sexual immorality," they said. "We have one Father—God" (8:41). Consequently, the circumstances around Jesus's birth suggested to his enemies that Joseph was not Jesus's biological father. While this is not an affirmation of the virgin birth, it does suggest that rumors circulated concerning Jesus's parents. Another possible allusion to questions surrounding Mary's conception was when the people of Nazareth described Jesus as "the son of Mary," implying Joseph was not his biological father (Mark 6:3). This would not have been an affirmation of his virginal conception, but a statement about the fact that Mary was pregnant before she "officially" married Joseph. While references to Jesus's virginal conception outside Luke's and Matthew's Gospels are few, the Lukan and Matthean statements are very clear. The issue is whether one believes the biblical accounts of the virgin birth or rejects them. A high view of Scripture and a belief in the sovereignty of God result in a belief in the virgin birth.

---

[12] This verse will be examined more fully in its Matthean context.

John Frame offers several reasons why a belief in the virgin birth is important.[13] First, as we have seen, Scripture clearly teaches the virgin birth of Jesus. For one to deny the truthfulness of the virgin birth is to deny the truthfulness of Scripture. Second, the virgin birth explains how Jesus can be both fully God and fully man. His deity suggests that his sinlessness and his humanity means he is one of us, but without sin. Jesus's sinlessness as the new head of humanity and as the atoning lamb of God is essential to our salvation (Rom 5:18–19; 2 Cor 5:21; 7:26–7; 1 Pet 2:22–24).

So the virgin birth is not a "tack on" to the Christian faith. The virgin birth is an essential doctrine teaching how God's Son is an all-sufficient Savior. As God, he was born without sin. As man, he never sinned and lived in perfect obedience to the Father. The only way he could die to redeem sinners was to be a human being. The only way he could be sinless was to be divine. The author of Hebrews adds two important implications of Christ's sinlessness as the God-man.

> For we do not have a high priest who is unable to sympathize with our weaknesses, but one who has been tempted in every way as we are, yet without sin. (Heb 4:15)

> For this is the kind of high priest we need: holy, innocent, undefiled, separated from sinners, and exalted above the heavens. He doesn't need to offer sacrifices every day, as high priests do—first for their own sins, then for those

---

[13] The following points are a summary of the implications of the virgin birth in John M. Frame, "Virgin Birth of Christ," in *Evangelical Dictionary of Theology*, ed. Walter A. Elwell, 2nd ed. (Grand Rapids: Baker, 2001), 1249–50.

of the people. He did this once for all time when he offered himself. (Heb 7:26–27)

A Dramatic Announcement: Savior, Son, and King (1:28–37)

While one cannot be certain where Gabriel appeared to Mary, it's likely the meeting took place in her parents' home. If Mary was like many young ladies, she had thoughts of what her married life would be like. As a carpenter, Joseph would be capable of making suitable furniture for a young family. Mary probably dreamed of the children they would have and the beauty of raising them with Joseph. Sometimes our dreams never come true, and sometimes they are better than we could have ever thought possible. Mary, likely, would not have imagined giving birth to Israel's Messiah or seen her life unfolding as it did.

Mary's story begins with her encounter with an angel. She was naturally quite startled and fearful (vv. 28–30). Mary's fear, however, was not the result of Gabriel's sudden and unexpected appearance, but the angel's surprising greeting, "But she was deeply troubled by this statement, wondering what kind of greeting this could be" (v. 29). After the initial greeting, Gabriel informed Mary that she was the object of God's favor (*charitoō*) and the Lord's presence was with her.[14]

For generations, the Jewish people had waited for the arrival of the one Gabriel described. The angel's words ("Now listen: You will conceive and give birth to a son") echo Isa 7:14.[15] The passage

---

[14] Garland, *Luke*, 79.

[15] Strauss, *Luke*, 15.

reads, "Therefore, the Lord himself will give you a sign: See, the virgin will conceive, have a son, and name him Immanuel."[16] Just as with Zechariah, Gabriel instructed Mary what name to give her son. The name "Jesus" ("Yahweh saves") is the Greek equivalent of the Hebrew *Yeshua* ("Joshua"). Luke, unlike Matthew, does not provide the meaning of the name (Matt 1:21). Gabriel informed Mary that her child would be both great and "Son of the Most High." While John the Baptist would be great in "the sight of the Lord," Jesus would be great without any qualifying epithet.

The title "Most High" (*hypsistos*) is used in both the Old Testament (Gen 14:18–20; 2 Sam 22:14; Ps 46:4; 91:1) and the New Testament (Luke 1:32, 35, 76; 6:35; 8:28; Heb 7:1) to refer to God.[17] When Gabriel spoke of Jesus as "Son of the Most High," Luke's readers would have understood the reference to be Jesus's fulfillment of the Messianic promises and his divine Sonship. Mary, however, would have likely understood the term only along the lines of Messiahship. The Gospel of Luke refers to Jesus's sonship at crucial moments. At Jesus's baptism, God the Father announced Jesus to be his "beloved Son" (3:22). Satan acknowledged Jesus's divine sonship in Jesus's wilderness temptations (4:3, 9). Demons confessed Jesus to be "the Son of God" before he silenced them (4:41). At the transfiguration, God again pronounced Jesus to be his Son ("this is my Son, my Chosen One") (9:35). Luke wanted his readers to understand that Jesus was the divine Messiah.

---

[16] Isaiah 7:14 will be examined more fully in chapter 7, where we discuss Matt 1:18–25.

[17] See Bock, *Luke*, 1:113–15, for a thorough discussion on the title "Son of the Most High."

There can be no mistaking Jesus's Messianic identity when Gabriel informed Mary that Jesus will sit on David's throne (v. 32). Verses 32–33 echo God's covenant with David.

> "The LORD declares to you: The LORD himself will make a house for you. When your time comes and you rest with your ancestors, I will raise up after you your descendant, who will come from your body, and I will establish his kingdom. He is the one who will build a house for my name, and I will establish the throne of his kingdom forever." (2 Sam 7:11–13)

A promise made to David, approximately nine hundred years earlier, was now being fulfilled in Christ's birth. The idea of an "eternal kingdom" is found in both 2 Samuel and Daniel.

> "Your house and kingdom will endure before me forever, and your throne will be established forever." (2 Sam 7:16)

> He was given dominion
> and glory and a kingdom,
> so that those of every people,
> nation, and language
> should serve him.
> His dominion is an everlasting dominion
> that will not pass away,
> and his kingdom is one
> that will not be destroyed. (Dan 7:14)

Mary clearly understood Gabriel's words would come to pass before the consummation of her marriage to Joseph. On the surface, Mary's question ("How can this be, since I have not had sexual relations with a man?") sounds very much like Zechariah's question ("How can I know this? For I am an old man, and my wife is well along in years."). Yet Gabriel's message to Zechariah had biblical precedent. What Gabriel told Mary was something that had never happened in human history. Mary's question was not a question of doubt concerning God's ability for her to become pregnant, but how she could conceive before the consummation of her marriage to Joseph. [18]

The virginal conception was the result of the powerful working of the Holy Spirit. Gabriel stated, "The Holy Spirit will come upon you, and the power of the Most High will overshadow you" (v. 35). Readers familiar with the Old Testament would think immediately of the imagery from Gen 1:2, "Now the earth was formless and empty, darkness covered the surface of the watery depths, and the Spirit of God was hovering over the surface of the waters." Just as God's Spirit filled the emptiness at the beginning of creation, so the Spirit filled Mary when she conceived Jesus. The "power of the Most High" is a circumlocution for the powerful working of the Spirit. The verb translated "come upon" (*eperchomai*) is used in Acts 1:8 to describe the Holy Spirit coming on believers at Pentecost.[19] While God's Spirit came on prophets, priests, and kings in the Old Covenant, in the New Covenant every believer is indwelt by God's Spirit.

Gabriel's use of the term "overshadow" (*episkiazō*) is also an interesting word. The verb is used in Exod 40:35 referring to God's Shekinah glory "overshadowing" the tabernacle in a cloud. The Shekinah glory of God is the manifestation of the presence

---

[18] Bock, *Luke*, 1:118. See also Garland, *Luke*, 81. Much scholarly debate has occurred over Mary's question. For a summary of the debate, see Bock, Luke, 1:118–21.

[19] Strauss, *Luke*, 16.

and power of God among his people. When the cloud of God's presence filled the tabernacle, God was present among his people in a particularly powerful way. All of this to say, the virginal conception was the powerful work of God, and God alone.

Gabriel's statement, "For nothing will be impossible with God" (v. 37), deserves to be printed in gold letters in every Bible. The statement is a theological affirmation repeated throughout the Scriptures. When Abraham and Sarah thought Sarah's ability to conceive a child was impossible, an angel told Abraham, "Is anything impossible for the LORD? At the appointed time I will come back to you, and in about a year she will have a son" (Gen 18:14). The prophet Jeremiah states the same truth this way, "Oh, Lord GOD! You yourself made the heavens and earth by your great power and with your outstretched arm. Nothing is too difficult for you!" (Jer 32:17). Later in the same chapter, God said to Jeremiah, "Look, I am the LORD, the God over every creature. Is anything too difficult for me?" (32:27). After Jesus told his disciples it is easier for a camel to go through the eye of a needle than for a rich person to be saved, they responded in astonishment, "Then who can be saved?" Jesus replied, "With man this is impossible, but with God all things are possible" (Matt 19:25–26). Jesus again confirmed the truth of God's ability to perform all his holy will when Jesus prayed in the garden, "And he said, '*Abba*, Father! All things are possible for you. Take this cup away from me. Nevertheless, not what I will, but what you will'" (Mark 14:36). God is sovereign and will accomplish all his plans. God can enable an elderly barren woman (Elizabeth) to conceive a child through the normal sexual relationship with her husband and a virgin (Mary) to conceive a child by the powerful working of the Holy Spirit. The truth that nothing is impossible with God remains true today. God's plans for his people will not be stopped, deterred, or hindered. God can be trusted to accomplish what he promises his people in his Word.

If any doubts existed in Mary's mind, they must have been demolished when she learned of Elizabeth's pregnancy (v. 36).[20] The reference to the "sixth month" of Elizabeth's pregnancy provides insight to the approximate length of time between these events and Elizabeth's conception (Luke 1:25). Mary's familial relationship to Elizabeth is left vague. For instance, Luke does not use the term "cousin" (*anepsios*) as Paul does when he writes of Mark's relationship with Barnabas (Col 4:10). Instead, Luke's use of the term translated "relative" (*syngenis*) is found nowhere else in the New Testament. While the exact specificity of Elizabeth and Mary's family relationship is unclear, what is obvious is that they were related.

A Courageous Embrace of God's Dangerous Will (1:38)

Mary embraced God's plan for her life without hesitation. While she could not have understood the full implications of what lay ahead for her and her son, she knew she could trust God's providence for her life.[21] For Luke's readers, Mary portrays a model disciple in her unreserved willingness to be God's servant. Her own plans, whatever they may have been, were willingly set aside to accept God's plan. Although she was quite young, Mary took Prov 16:9 with the utmost seriousness, "We can make our plans, but the LORD determines our steps" (16:9 NLT).

---

[20] Bock, *Luke*, 1:126.
[21] Garland, *Luke*, 83.

Final Reflections

While this passage has several truths to focus our attention on, two will be highlighted. First, Mary demonstrated great faith in God. What she heard from Gabriel must have astonished her. Faith did not make God big, but the God in whom Mary trusted is a big and all-powerful, loving God. Mary's faith in God infused her life, enabling her to believe that God can do what he says he will do. Mary embraced Gabriel's words, "Nothing will be impossible with God" (Luke 1:37). The Christian life is a battle against the world, the flesh, and the devil. American culture is becoming more hostile to the Christian faith. More and more countries around the world are intensifying their persecution of believers and passing stringent laws against conversion to Christianity. Believers could easily become discouraged about living for God's glory in our day. Inscribe Gabriel's words on your mind, "Nothing will be impossible with God."

Second, we must not leave this passage without bringing our focus back to Jesus. We must remember the central character in this passage is not the angel Gabriel or Mary, but Jesus. Jesus's name reflects his mission—to bring God's salvation to a lost world. Every time we read the name "Jesus," we need to remember "Yahweh saves!" God saves not the self-righteous but sinners (Luke 5:32) like the immoral woman and Zacchaeus (Luke 7:36–50; 19:1–10). Jesus came to "seek and to save the lost" (Luke 19:10). As the apostles preached, "There is salvation in no one else, for there is no other name under heaven given to people by which we must be saved" (Acts 4:12). The worship of Jesus during the Christmas season should inspire us to embrace his mission of taking the gospel to those in need of salvation. Those who understand this mission love the meaning of Christmas the most and will gladly spread the good news of the gospel.

A Christmas Hymn of Response

Joy to the world! the Lord is come;
Let earth receive her King;
Let ev'ry heart prepare Him room,
And heav'n and nature sing,
And heav'n and nature sing,
And heav'n, and heav'n, and nature sing.

Joy to the earth! the Savior reigns;
Let men their songs employ;
While fields and floods, rocks, hills, and plains
Repeat the sounding joy,
Repeat the sounding joy,
Repeat, repeat, the sounding joy.

No more let sins and sorrows grow,
Nor thorns infest the ground;
He comes to make His blessings flow
Far as the curse is found,
Far as the curse is found,
Far as, far as, the curse is found.

He rules the world with truth and grace,
And makes the nations prove
The glories of His righteousness,
And wonders of His love,
And wonders of His love,
And wonders, wonders, of His love.[22]

---

[22] Isaac Watts, "Joy to the World! The Lord Is Come," 1719, *Baptist Hymnal*, #87.

Taking a Deeper Dive: False Teachings on Mary

While Mary is to be honored for her bravery and faith, she is certainly not to be venerated and worshiped. Mary is a human being and not divine. Attempts have been made through the ages to exalt Mary to an unbiblical position, one she would not have wanted. Traditional Roman Catholic teaching concerning Mary centers on several erroneous doctrines.[23] One is the belief in Mary's Perpetual Virginity. This doctrine teaches that Mary remained a virgin her entire life. Catholic teaching bases this doctrine on Mary's words in Luke 1:34, "How can this be, since I have not had sexual relations with a man?" This understanding of the verse suggests Mary took a lifelong vow of celibacy and never engaged in a sexual union with Joseph. A more reasonable interpretation of Mary's words is to understand them to mean she is presently a virgin and wonders how she could become pregnant before the consummation of her marriage to Joseph. Furthermore, there are clear references in the New Testament to Jesus's brothers and sisters (Matt 13:55–56; Mark 3:31–34; 6:3). Luke writes in Acts 1:14, "All these were continually devoting themselves with one mind to prayer, along with the women, and Mary the mother of Jesus, and with his brothers." Those who hold to the perpetual virginity of Mary suggest the references to Jesus's brothers and sisters should be understood to be cousins or distant relations. However, if this is the case, why didn't the evangelists use the Greek term for cousins (*anepsios*)? Paul used

---

[23] For a complete discussion on Roman Catholic doctrine, see Greg Allison, *Roman Catholic Theology and Practice: An Evangelical Assessment* (Wheaton, IL: Crossway, 2014).

the term when referring to Mark's relationship with Barnabas (Col 4:10). If they were more distant relatives, then the writers could have used the term Luke used describing the relationship between Mary and Elizabeth in 1:36 (*sungenes*). Both Gospel writers used the most common term when referring to Jesus's brothers (*adelphos*) and sisters (*adelphē*). In addition, Paul wrote concerning James, "But I didn't see any of the other apostles except James, the Lord's brother" (Gal 1:19).The biblical evidence for the perpetual virginity of Mary does not exist.

A second erroneous teaching concerning Mary is known as the Immaculate Conception. This doctrine teaches that Mary was conceived without original sin. Catholic theologians base this doctrine on a misunderstanding of Luke 1:28: "Greetings, favored woman! The Lord is with you." This teaching clearly contradicts the Bible's teaching on original sin (Rom 3:23). The apostle John wrote, "If we say, 'We have no sin,' we are deceiving ourselves, and the truth is not in us. If we confess our sins, he is faithful and righteous to forgive us our sins and to cleanse us from all unrighteousness. If we say, 'We have not sinned,' we make him a liar, and his word is not in us" (1 John 1:8–10). There is no biblical support to teach the sinlessness of Mary.

The Assumption of Mary is a third false teaching concerning Mary. This doctrine suggests that Mary did not die but was taken bodily from earth to heaven. The thought is that Mary was conceived without original sin and therefore she would not die because of her sin. Her death would be attributed to her old age if she died at all. Obviously, there is no biblical foundation for this doctrine. The Bible seems to teach that both Enoch and Elijah were taken to heaven without dying (Gen 5:24; 2 Kgs 2:11). Nothing of the sort is said of Mary. The belief is based solely on church dogma and lacks any scriptural support.

Despite these heretical teachings concerning Mary, she remains a model of faithfulness to God. Faithfulness to God can be dangerous. While none of us will be in Mary's exact situation, we must be willing to embrace God's call and follow his will wherever he leads us, however dangerous that might be. The swiftness of Mary's response revealed the depth of her trust in God's goodness. May our response to God's call be just as swift.

CHAPTER 5

THE SONGS OF SPIRIT-FILLED WOMEN

LUKE 1:39–56

> My soul magnifies the Lord,
> and my spirit rejoices in God my Savior.
> —Luke 1:46–47

After the annunciations to Zechariah and Mary, the next major event in Luke's story is the meeting of the two mothers—Elizabeth and Mary. The scene shifts from Bethlehem to a small village in the Judean countryside. Our familiarity with the encounter between these two women weakens its potential impact on us. God is bringing together events planned before the foundation of the world. Here, the forerunner of the Messiah is about to leap in his mother's womb the moment he is in his Lord's presence (who is in his own mother's womb). Even in his prenatal state, John is fulfilling his calling.

Elizabeth's blessing of Mary captures the magnitude of the moment, and Mary's song encapsulates the hope of the ages coming to pass. The encounter between these two women demonstrates the continuing work of the Holy Spirit and anticipates John's future acknowledgment of Jesus's superiority to him (Luke 3:16–17). The passage falls into two parts: Elizabeth's blessing of Mary (vv. 39–45) and Mary's song of praise to God (vv. 46–55).

Elizabeth's Prophetic Blessing (1:39–45)

At some point, shortly after Mary's encounter with Gabriel, she traveled to visit Elizabeth and Zechariah (v. 39). The journey from Nazareth to the Judean hill country, somewhere near Jerusalem, is approximately seventy miles, depending on the exact location. The journey would have taken Mary four to five days. While the precise location of her relative's home is unknown, the traditional site is *Ain Karim*, located five miles west of Jerusalem. We are not told if she made the journey alone. If she had travelled alone, the journey would not have been safe for a young lady of her age. She must have felt a sense of urgency to visit Elizabeth since she made the trip in haste (*spoudē*) (v. 39).[1] At the time of Gabriel's appearance to Mary, Elizabeth was six months pregnant. Mary remained three months with her relatives, likely leaving shortly after John's birth.

Mary greeted Elizabeth when Mary entered her home (v. 40). Mary's greeting is mentioned three times in the passage (vv. 40–41, 44).[2] When Elizabeth heard Mary's greeting, Elizabeth's unborn baby leaped within her womb, and she was filled with the Holy Spirit (v. 41). Earlier, Luke indicated that John was filled with the Holy Spirit while still in Elizabeth's

---

[1] For other possible nuances to the term see David E. Garland, *Luke*, Zondervan Exegetical Commentary on the New Testament (Grand Rapids: Zondervan, 2011), 91.

[2] Garland, *Luke*, 92.

womb (1:15). The verb translated "leaped" (*skirtaō*) is an expression of joy (cf. Mal 4:2). As a result of the Spirit's illumination, Elizabeth recognized Mary was pregnant with the Messiah ("my Lord") (v. 43). No mention is made of Zechariah since he remained mute and played no role in this encounter.

As a result of the Spirit's filling, Elizabeth spoke prophetic words regarding Mary's role in the drama of redemption as "the mother of my Lord." Elizabeth's comments to Mary begin and end with the word "blessed." Most English translations, however, obscure the fact that two different Greek words are used. In verse 42, the Greek word *eulogeō* is used twice. The term refers to God's blessing of Mary and her unborn child. Both uses of the word "blessed" are passive participles indicating what God has done for Mary and her child.[3] In verse 45, the word is *makarios* and expresses how others regard Mary as blessed by God, acknowledging what God has done for her (cf. Luke 6:20–22). Mary was not commended because of her good "luck" but for the faith she demonstrated when she took God at his word. The first use of the word "Lord" being applied to Jesus is by Elizabeth (v. 43). Elizabeth, filled with the Spirit, likely spoke better than she knew.

One final thought before we move on is the astounding fact that not the slightest hint of jealousy can be heard in Elizabeth's words. Not only would Mary play a more substantial role in salvation history than Elizabeth, but so would Mary's son. Elizabeth's response, however, is not surprising given the description of her and Zechariah earlier (Luke 1:5–7). Elizabeth's heart was filled with joy because God was at work, and she did not bother herself with matters of self-glory. We need more people in the church of Christ like Elizabeth.

---

[3] Garland, *Luke*, 92.

Worship from the Heart: Mary's
Magnificat (1:46–56)

This is the first of four famous "songs" (or hymns) in Luke's
Birth and Infancy narrative (cf. 1:67–79; 2:14; 2:29–32).[4] These
"hymns" are printed in poetic fashion in most English translations. This hymn is called the *Magnificat* from the opening verb
of the Latin Vulgate's translation.[5] The verb *megalynō* literally
means *magnify* or *glorify*. In this context, the hymn is an ascrip-
tion of praise to God. Two features in particular stand out in the
passage. First, the passage is filled with Old Testament quotes
and allusions. Thus, Mary's spontaneous praise exemplified her
deep devotion to Scripture. A second important theme is that
Mary worshiped a God who lifts up the poor and downtrodden
and casts down the rich and the proud (the Great Reversal).

Mary's hymn echoes many aspects of Hannah's praise to God
for her child in 1 Sam 2:1–10.[6] A brief comparison of the two
women and their prayers will demonstrate their similarities.[7] Both
Hannah and Mary identified themselves as "the Lord's servants"
(1 Sam 1:11; Luke 1:38, 48). Both Hannah and Mary experienced

---

[4] For an extensive treatment on these hymns, see Stephen Farris, *The
Hymns of Luke's Infancy Narratives*, Biblical Studies: Bloomsbury Academic
Collections (New York: Bloomsbury Academic, 1985).

[5] For a full discussion on the background of the *Magnificat* and its
historicity Darrell L. Bock, *Luke*, Baker Exegetical Commentary on the
New Testament, 2 vols. (Grand Rapids: Baker Academic, 1994), 1:142–47.

[6] Bock, *Luke*, 1:148. For a recent discussion on the relationship
between Hannah's prayer and Mary's praise, see Benjamin L. Gladd, *From
the Manger to the Throne: A Theology of Luke*, A New Testament Theology
(Wheaton, IL: Crossway, 2022), 40–44.

[7] I gleaned this helpful comparison from Gladd, *From the Manger to
the Throne*, 40–44.

a miraculous conception. While Hannah conceived a child with her husband after suffering greatly with infertility (1 Sam 1:5), Mary conceived a child as a virgin (Luke 1:34–35). Both women offered praise to God for the birth (or future birth) of their sons (1 Sam 2:1–10; Luke 1:46–55). Both women praised God who exalts the humble and brings down the haughty (1 Sam 2:6–8; Luke 1:52). A crucial difference between Mary's praise and Hannah's prayer is that the messianic themes are more distinct in Mary's *Magnificat*.

One may wonder how Luke came to know what Mary and Elizabeth said to one another. We should not dismiss the possibility that Luke may have spoken to Mary or those close to her. In Luke 2:19 and 2:51, Luke indicates Mary "treasured" (*syntēreō*) these events in her heart, which carries the thought of preserving a memory. We know from Luke's prologue that he investigated these events thoroughly, using both eyewitness testimonies and reliable written sources (1:1–4).

Below is a sample of the Old Testament references found in Mary's *Magnificat*. As mentioned above, many of the texts of the references are included because by reading them you will feel more of the impact of Mary's song. Read them out loud, and you will feel even more of the spiritual weight of her words.

Mary Praises God for His Goodness to Her (1:46–48)

The *Magnificat* can be divided into four stanzas (strophes).[8] In the opening stanza, Mary praises God for his goodness to her.

---

[8] My understanding of the structure and movement of the hymn is dependent on Walter L. Liefeld and David W. Pao, "Luke," in *Luke–Acts*, ed. Tremper Longman III and David E Garland, rev. ed., vol. 10 of *The Expositor's Bible Commentary* (Grand Rapids: Zondervan, 2007), 63–64.

The opening lines are an example of Hebrew parallelism, where the second line is a repetition of the former line but expressed in synonymous words. Mary's soul/spirit magnifies/rejoices in the Lord/God. The verb "magnifies" (*megalynō*) carries the thought of "enlarge" or "amplify" and thus to magnify or to praise. The reason Mary's soul magnifies and rejoices in God is because he has shown favor towards her and done great things for her, despite her humble status. As a result, all generations will call her blessed. Mary's words are not intended to evoke veneration of her but to acknowledge that she is the recipient of God's powerful work in her life.[9] A few of the references that give insight into Mary's thoughts are set forth below.

> I will boast in the Lord; the humble will hear and be glad. Proclaim the Lord's greatness with me; let us exalt his name together. (Ps 34:2–3)

> But I will look to the Lord; I will wait for the God of my salvation. My God will hear me. (Mic 7:7)

> He will receive blessing from the Lord, and righteousness from the God of his salvation. (Ps 24:5)

> Guide me in your truth and teach me, for you are the God of my salvation; I wait for you all day long. (Ps 25:5)

When we magnify the Lord, we do not make God bigger, but we focus the attention of our heart on our *big* God. When God's people magnify him, they enlarge him in their minds and hearts. The better we know God from the Scriptures, the better equipped we are to worship him rightly. Mary's worship teaches

---

[9] Also see David E. Garland, *Luke*, Zondervan Exegetical Commentary on the New Testament (Grand Rapids: Zondervan, 2011), 95.

us that our worship should be infused with high thoughts of God grounded in Scriptural revelation.

Mary Praises God for His Holiness, Power, and Mercy (1:49–50)

Mary shifts her focus from gratitude to God for his goodness to her, to praise of God's attributes (vv. 49b–50). She focuses on God's power, holiness, and mercy. In the opening line of v. 49, she refers to God as the "Mighty One." Mary's understanding of God's character is firmly rooted in the Old Testament. A few Old Testament references to God as "the Mighty One" can help us better understand Mary's thought.

> Yet his bow remained steady,
> and his strong arms were made agile
> by the hands of the Mighty One of Jacob,
> by the name of the Shepherd, the Rock of Israel.
>   (Gen 49:24)

The Mighty One, God, the LORD! The Mighty One, God, the LORD! He knows, and may Israel also know. Do not spare us today, if it was in rebellion or treachery against the LORD. (Josh 22:22)

> Therefore the Lord GOD of Armies,
> the Mighty One of Israel, declares:
> "Ah, I will get even with my foes;
> I will take revenge against my enemies." (Isa 1:24)

> For a child will be born for us,
> a son will be given to us,
> and the government will be on his shoulders.

He will be named
Wonderful Counselor, Mighty God,
Eternal Father, Prince of Peace. (Isa 9:6)

The term "mighty" is a translation of a Hebrew word (*gibbor*), which carries the idea of "strength, power, hero, or warrior." Isaiah 9:6, which is quoted above, tells us that Jesus is the God of might, strength, and power. The baby born in Bethlehem is God, our Mighty Warrior. This sweet and innocent child being held in Mary's arms will one day rule the nations. By meditating on these verses speaking of God as the Mighty One, we will be encouraged to trust God more fully in the difficulties of life. These verses encourage us to believe that "nothing will be impossible with God," the Mighty One.

Another divine attribute of God that Mary praises is his holiness. The following are Old Testament references highlighting this thought.

For I am the LORD your God, so you must consecrate yourselves and be holy because I am holy. (Lev 11:44)

Speak to the entire Israelite community and tell them: Be holy because I, the LORD your God, am holy. (Lev 19:2)

You are to be holy to me because I, the LORD, am holy, and I have set you apart from the nations to be mine. (Lev 20:26)

Surely our shield belongs to the LORD,
our king to the Holy One of Israel. (Ps 89:18)

He has sent redemption to his people.
He has ordained his covenant forever.

His name is holy and awe-inspiring. (Ps 111:9)

These verses remind us that the God we worship and serve has called his people to live holy lives in an unholy world. God's mercy is demonstrated throughout the Scriptures. Below are a few references to God's mercy.

> And the LORD said, "I will cause all my goodness to pass in front of you, and I will proclaim my name, the LORD, in your presence. I will have mercy on whom I will have mercy, and I will have compassion on whom I will have compassion." (Exod 33:19 NIV)

> But from eternity to eternity
> the LORD's faithful love is toward those who fear him,
> and his righteousness toward the grandchildren. (Ps
>   103:17)

> Let the wicked forsake their ways and the unrighteous their thoughts. Let them turn to the LORD, and he will have mercy on them, and to our God, for he will freely pardon. (Isa 55:7 NIV)

> Who is a God like You, who pardons wrongdoing
> And passes over a rebellious act of the remnant of His
>   possession?
> He does not retain His anger forever, Because He
>   delights in mercy. (Mic 7:18 NASB)

No doubt these verses and others like them filled Mary's mind and reminded her of God's power, holiness, and mercy. A major point being made in these verses is that everything that is transpiring is commensurate with God's character.

Mary Praises God for Exalting the Humble (1:51–53)

In the third stanza, Mary highlights God's sovereignty and mercy demonstrated in reversing the social positions of the rich and powerful with the weak and poor (vv. 51–52). Mary declares that God is clearly on the side of the underdog. God's strength is personified in the term "arm" (*brachiōn*). The "arm of the Lord" is a personification of the power of God. An example can be seen in Exod 6:6, "Therefore tell the Israelites: I am the LORD, and I will bring you out from the forced labor of the Egyptians and rescue you from slavery to them. I will redeem you with an outstretched arm and great acts of judgment." On the one hand, God has demonstrated his strong arm in scattering the proud, bringing down the powerful, and sending the rich away empty. On the other hand, God's power is equally demonstrated by lifting the humble and filling the hungry with good things. While these mighty acts of God remain in the future, Mary is so certain they will take place that she speaks as if they have already occurred.[10]

Mary Praises God for His Mercy to Israel (1:54–55)

In the fourth stanza, Mary turns her attention to God's present mercy toward Israel (vv. 54–55). Once again, Mary speaks prophetically, using past tense verbs to speak of future events. God's great help and mercy refer to the coming of Israel's Messiah, which fulfills God's promises to Abraham and his descendants. Earlier, Gabriel referred to the Davidic covenant (1:33), and now

---

[10] For a full discussion on the various interpretations of these aorist tense verbs see Bock, *Luke*, 1:154–55. Bock understands them to be prophetic aorists "portraying the ultimate eschatological events tied to Jesus' final victory." I understand the verbs to be referring to Jesus's first coming.

Mary references the Abrahamic covenant.[11] The following are examples of God's promises to Abraham and his descendants.

> "By myself I have sworn," this is the Lord's declaration: "Because you have done this thing and have not withheld your only son, I will indeed bless you and make your offspring as numerous as the stars of the sky and the sand on the seashore. Your offspring will possess the city gates of their enemies. And all the nations of the earth will be blessed by your offspring because you have obeyed my command." (Gen 22:16–18)

> Therefore I will give thanks to you among the nations,
>   Lord;
> I will sing praises about your name.
> He is a tower of salvation for his king;
> he shows loyalty to his anointed,
> to David and his descendants forever. (2 Sam 22:50–51)

> For I will declare,
> "Faithful love is built up forever;
> you establish your faithfulness in the heavens."
> The Lord said,
> "I have made a covenant with my chosen one;
> I have sworn an oath to David my servant:
> 'I will establish your offspring forever
> and build up your throne for all generations.'" (Ps 89:2–4)

> Who is a God like you,
> forgiving iniquity and passing over rebellion

---

[11] Other Lukan references to Abraham are Luke 1:73; 3:8; 16:24; Acts 3:25; 7:5–6.

for the remnant of his inheritance?
He does not hold on to his anger forever
because he delights in faithful love.
He will again have compassion on us;
he will vanquish our iniquities.
You will cast all our sins
into the depths of the sea.
You will show loyalty to Jacob
and faithful love to Abraham,
as you swore to our ancestors
from days long ago. (Mic 7:18–20)

The depth of Mary's understanding of Scripture is staggering. Whether Mary could read is not known. It would not have been unusual for her to be illiterate. What is clear is that Mary knew the Scriptures, learning them in her local synagogue and in her parents' home. The truths of God's Word had taken root in her heart. When she opened her lips in praise to God, flowing out of her mouth came that which filled her heart (Matt 12:34).

Mary's knowledge and understanding of Scripture should challenge parents to instruct their children in the truths of Scripture and to have their children involved in a church that preaches the Bible. Never underestimate the power of God's Spirit to work in the heart of your children through God's Word.

Final Reflections

As events continue to unfold, we see the age of the Spirit was dawning. Elizabeth was filled with the Spirit and spoke words that summarized realities of which she was unaware. As a result of divine illumination, Elizabeth pronounced that Mary was pregnant with God's Messiah. These words reflected God's continued superintendence of events as they unfolded. The birth of Christ was a divine plan being fulfilled by God's providence and being made known through inspired prophecy.

Another important truth in this passage is how God-honoring worship is fueled by the Spirit and the Word. Spirit-filled worship without a biblical underpinning falls short of worshiping in Spirit and truth. The words the church sings when it gathers for corporate worship, or the songs believers sing in private worship, should be saturated in scriptural content. Our worship—whether more contemporary or traditional in style—must be theologically rich and biblically faithful if it is to be God-honoring. Mary's song demonstrated theological fidelity, was God-focused, and is a model of heartfelt worship. Mary worshiped God for who he is and what he has done in the past, what he is doing in the present, and what he will do in the future. At every turn in her *Magnificat*, she extolled God—his power, holiness, mercy, his concern for the outcast, and his disgust for the proud. Genuine worship is both taught and caught. We must teach our churches that the content of biblical worship is the person and work of Christ. Furthermore, biblical worship requires that our hearts, minds, and mouths be engaged. When churches worship God faithfully, they join their voice with the voices of the angels of heaven.

Finally, the most important truths in the passage center on our triune God. First, as mentioned above, the Holy Spirit filled Elizabeth and enabled her to know things she could not possibly have known. How did Elizabeth know Mary was pregnant? How did Elizabeth know that Mary's child was the Messiah-King ("the mother of my Lord"). Second, God the Father is the God of the impossible. He is completely holy,

all-powerful, and filled with mercy. God the Father's plans
are in the process of being fulfilled. Third, we are discovering how the Scriptures find their ultimate fulfillment in Jesus.
As these events unfolded, those involved reached back to the
past to describe what was taking place in the present. When
Mary sang, "He has helped his servant Israel, remembering his
mercy to Abraham and his descendants forever" (vv. 55–56),
she was acknowledging that the child to be born to her would
fulfill the Abrahamic promises. In addition, when Mary sang,
"He has satisfied the hungry with good things and sent the
rich away empty" (v. 53), she was speaking of more than food;
she was speaking of the longing of the human heart. She was
singing of the emptiness of the human soul. Mary spoke of
One who would declare himself to be "the bread of life" (John
6:35). Jesus went on to say, "No one who comes to me will ever
be hungry, and no one who believes in me will ever be thirsty
again." Mary sang of the One who would fulfill the Abrahamic
covenant and cast down the proud and the haughty but who
would give himself to the humble and meek and feed the spiritually hungry.

A Christmas Hymn of Response

Angels we have heard on high,
Sweetly singing o'er the plains;
And the mountains in reply,
Echoing their joyous strains.

Chorus:
Gloria in excelsis Deo!
Gloria in excelsis Deo!

Shepherds, why this jubilee?
Why your joyous strains prolong?
What the gladsome tidings be
Which inspire your heav'nly song?

[Chorus]

Come to Bethlehem, and see
Him whose birth the angels sing;
Come, adore on bended knee
Christ the Lord the newborn King.

[Chorus]

See Him in a manger laid,
Whom the choirs of angels praise;
Mary, Joseph, lend your aid,
While our hearts in love we raise.

[Chorus][12]

Taking a Deeper Dive: The Great Reversal

In many ways, Luke's Gospel is about a revolution, not a military revolution but a spiritual one. Mary's song indicates that God is turning the world upside-down with the coming of the Messiah. Rather than the rich being favored over the poor, God will feed the poor, and those who are financially rich are in grave danger. In Luke 1:53, Mary magnifies the Lord: "He has filled the hungry with good things and sent the rich away empty." When

---

[12] Henry W. Longfellow, "Angels We Have Heard on High," 1862, *Baptist Hymnal*, #100.

Jesus read from Isaiah in the Nazareth synagogue he stated, "The
Spirit of the LORD . . . has anointed me to bring good news to
the poor" (Luke 4:18 NLT). In Jesus's Sermon on the Plain, he
said to his disciples, "Blessed are you who are poor, because the
kingdom of God is yours. Blessed are you who are hungry now,
because you will be filled. Blessed are you who weep now because
you will laugh . . . But woe to you who are rich, for you have
received your comfort. Woe to you who are now full, for you will
be hungry. Woe to you who are now laughing, for you will mourn
and weep" (6:20–21, 24–25). At a dinner party, Jesus told the host
that instead of simply inviting family members and friends, he
should invite the poor, lame, and blind (14:12–13). In the parable
of the great banquet, when the master learned that those origi-
nally invited refused to attend, he instructed his servants to invite
the poor, the crippled, the blind, and the lame (14:21).

In the parable of the rich fool, Jesus warned about the ever-
present danger of greed (12:15). In the parable of the unrighteous
steward, Jesus taught his disciples that they could not love God
and money (16:13). In the parable of the rich man and Lazarus,
Jesus taught that appearances can be deceiving. Lazarus, who
lived in poverty, was in a right relationship with God despite his
poverty, while the rich man who satisfied himself with worldly
pleasures in the end lost everything (16:19–31) much like the rich
fool. In a most memorable story, Luke described how Zacchaeus,
a wealthy tax collector, gave half of his goods to the poor and paid
back anyone he had defrauded four times as much (19:1–10).
Zacchaeus did the very things the rich young ruler was unwilling to do when invited to follow Jesus (18:18–23). No wonder
Jesus said, "How hard it is for those who have wealth to enter the
kingdom of God! For it is easier for a camel to go through the eye
of a needle than for a rich person to enter the kingdom of God"

(18:24–25). Jesus was speaking hyperbolically, using the image of the largest Palestinian animal (a camel) passing through the smallest Palestinian opening (the eye of a needle) as being easier than a rich person being saved. In response to the disciples' bewilderment, Jesus replied, "What is impossible with man is possible with God" (18:27). Jesus came into the world to save sinners— the rich and the poor. The ability of the wealthy to sense their need for God can be an extremely difficult task. Mary's song taps into the theme running throughout Luke's Gospel of the Great Reversal. Those whom the world considers insignificant and pushes to the fringe of society, Jesus came to save!

CHAPTER 6

THE SONG OF A SPIRIT-FILLED MAN

LUKE 1:57–80

> Blessed is the Lord, the God of Israel,
> because he has visited
> and provided redemption for his people.
> He has raised up a horn of salvation for us
> in the house of his servant David,
> just as he spoke by the mouth
> of his holy prophets in ancient times.
> —Luke 1:68–70

We move from Elizabeth and Mary to Zechariah. Zechariah had not spoken in nine months. For nine long months, he was unable to rejoice over the coming birth of his son. He was not able to describe in words the emotional experience of encountering Gabriel. Luke 1:57–80 can be divided into three sections: first, the birth, circumcision, and naming of John (vv. 57–66); second, Zechariah's *Benedictus* with the focus on the coming Messiah (vv. 67–75); and third, Zechariah's words concerning his son, John (vv. 76–79). The final verse summarizes John growing up in the wilderness (v. 80).

Birth, Circumcision, and Naming of John (1:57–66)

Luke does not record any event covering the three-month period from Mary's arrival to John's birth (v. 57). One can hardly imagine the late-night conversations between Elizabeth and Mary as they talked about the events from the preceding weeks. The scene depicting John's birth presents a small rural community of family and friends celebrating with the elderly couple over the birth of their son (v. 58). Gabriel's promise that many would rejoice at John's birth had come to pass (cf. 1:14).[1] For Elizabeth, the stigma of childlessness was finally erased.

In the following verses, Luke recounts the circumcision of the baby and his parents' determination to name him John. Every Jewish male was to be circumcised on the eighth day following his birth (v. 59). God commanded Abraham and later the nation to circumcise every male child on the eighth day (Gen 17:9–14; Lev 12:3). Circumcision was a sign of the covenant. By circumcising John, the elderly couple once again demonstrated their faithfulness to God.

We are not told why the family waited until the circumcision to name their baby. In the Old Testament, the naming of a child normally took place at birth (Gen 4:1; 25:25–26).[2] Earlier, Gabriel instructed Zechariah to name the child John. The text gives the

---

[1] Robert H. Stein, *Luke*, vol. 24, The New American Commentary (Nashville: B&H Academic, 1992), 97.

[2] Darrell L. Bock, *Luke*, Baker Exegetical Commentary on the New Testament 2 vols. (Grand Rapids: Baker Academic, 1994), 1:166.

impression that Zechariah had communicated this information to Elizabeth.[3] While family and friends assumed the baby would be named after his father or grandfather, Elizabeth insisted on the name "John" (v. 59). Those gathered sought to go around Elizabeth and find out what name Zechariah wanted for the baby (vv. 61–62). The crowd's use of signs to communicate with Zechariah suggests he was deaf as well as mute. Since Zechariah remained mute, he requested a writing tablet. Much to the surprise of those gathered, he wrote that the baby's name *is* John, and immediately (*parachrēma*) Zechariah's voice was restored (vv. 63–64).[4] The bystanders were filled with fear and bewilderment at the turn of events. The news surrounding the circumcision and naming of John spread throughout the region. Those present on that momentous day wondered what great plans God had in store for this child. The question was asked, "What then will this child become?" (v. 66). An excellent question! The answer to the question is found in Zechariah's prophecy in vv. 76–79.

Zechariah's Song: The *Benedictus* (1:67–79)

After the brief description of the birth, circumcision, and naming of John, Luke turns to a lengthy song intended to help readers understand further the significance of the events transpiring. The passage falls into three sections. The song focuses on the fulfillment of God's promises to David (vv. 68–71) and Abraham (vv. 72–75) and concludes with John's role in the unfolding of these events (vv. 76–79).[5]

---

[3] Stein, *Luke*, 97.

[4] Luke often uses the term "immediately" to describe how quickly Jesus's miracles took place (5:25; 8:44, 47, 55; 13:13; 18:43; 22:6; etc.).

[5] For helpful discussions on the Davidic Covenant, see Thomas R. Schreiner, *Covenant and God's Purpose for the World*, Short Studies

The Fulfillment of God's Promises to David (1:67–71)

Zechariah's prophecy was the result of his being filled with the Spirit (v. 67). Just as his wife, Elizabeth, had been filled with the Spirit when she encountered Mary, Zechariah's tongue was loosed, and he was filled with the Spirit. One can only imagine the shock of those gathered when hearing Zechariah suddenly speak. The reference to the Holy Spirit is another reminder that the coming of the Messiah inaugurated the age of the Spirit.

After nine months of silence, Zechariah's first words were filled with praise to God.[6] Zechariah's song is called the *Benedictus* (*eulogētos*), after the opening word in the Latin Vulgate translation of the passage. While Mary's song is more like a psalm, Zechariah's song is more prophetic in nature.[7] At the heart of Zechariah's words is the thought that God's ancient promises were being fulfilled. Much like Mary's *Magnificat*, Zechariah's *Benedictus* is filled with Old Testament quotations, allusions, and echoes.

Zechariah's opening words, "Blessed be the Lord," were a common way to introduce gratitude to God, especially in the

---

in Biblical Theology (Wheaton, IL: Crossway, 2017), 73–87; and Christopher H. Wright, *Knowing Jesus Through the Old Testament* (Downers Grove: IVP Academic, 1992), 88–93. For discussions on the Abrahamic Covenant, see Schreiner, *Covenant*, 41–57, and Wright, *Knowing Jesus*, 83–85.

[6] Often in Luke's Gospel and in Acts, praise is the response to the miraculous. For example, see Luke 5:26; 7:16; Acts 2:43; 19:17.

[7] In Peter's Pentecost sermon, he quoted Joel 2:29, "I will even pour out my Spirit on my servants in those days, both men and women and they will prophesy" (Acts 2:17–18).

psalms (41:13; 72:18; 106:48). In the opening section of the song, Zechariah speaks of the fulfillment of God's promises to David (vv. 68–71). Like Mary, Zechariah refers to Israel's redemption as though it has taken place: "He [God] has come . . . and redeemed . . . raised up a horn." Zechariah's words remind us that Jesus's birth fulfilled God's ancient promises to his people. The fact that God has "visited" (*episkeptomai*) his people echoes frequent Old Testament accounts of God coming to save or judge his people. The idea of God coming to Israel in grace and mercy can be seen in the following two verses.

> The people believed, and when they heard that the LORD had paid attention to them and that he had seen their misery, they knelt low and worshiped. (Exod 4:31)

> She [Naomi] and her daughters-in-law set out to return from the territory of Moab, because she had heard in Moab that the LORD had paid attention to his people's need by providing them food. (Ruth 1:6)

More important, the thought of God visiting his people to redeem (*lytrōsis*) them recalls God's powerful act of deliverance in the exodus from Egypt and the new exodus proclaimed by the prophets (for example, see Isa 43:19–20; 48:21; 52:11–12).[8] The thought of Israel's divine rescue from Egyptian bondage is stated in Deut 7:8, "But because the LORD loved you and kept the oath he swore to your ancestors, he brought you out with a strong hand and redeemed you from the place of slavery,

---

[8] Stein, *Luke*, 99, suggests that the coming of both Jesus and John should be considered a part of God's visitation of his people.

from the power of Pharaoh king of Egypt." The same thought is found in God's deliverance of his people from Babylonian bondage. Jeremiah 31:11 reads, "For the LORD has ransomed Jacob and redeemed him from the power of one stronger than he."

The act of redemption carries the thought of securing something, or someone, for freedom by the payment of a ransom. God came to visit and redeem his people in the person of his Son, Jesus Christ. Unfortunately, most of the Jewish nation at the time failed to recognize God's Son when he arrived. The apostle John wrote, "He [Jesus] came to his own, and his own people did not receive him" (John 1:11).

First-century Israel saw themselves once again in captivity, but this time to the Roman Empire. Many Jewish people expected the coming Messiah to be a militaristic warrior, like David.[9] The Messiah would set the nation free from Roman domination and establish an earthly kingdom. God's plan, however, was incomparably greater. God redeems his people from spiritual bondage to Satan, sin, and death.

In his *Benedictus*, Zechariah praises God for having raised up a "horn of salvation" (v. 69). Once again, Zechariah speaks as if a future event has already taken place, indicating the certainty of the event's occurrence. In the Old Testament, a horn often represents power and might. For example, in 2 Sam 22:3, David says, "My God, my rock where I seek refuge. My shield, the horn of my salvation, my stronghold, my refuge, and my Savior, you save me from violence." Another example can be found in Ezek 29:21, "In that day I will cause a horn to sprout for the

---

[9] See chapter 14, "The Old Testament Messianic Expectations of a Coming One."

house of Israel, and I will enable you to speak out among them. Then they will know that I am the LORD." The "horn of salvation" to be "raised up" is none other than God's Messiah, the one from the Davidic line ("in the house of his servant David").[10] From a human perspective, the lifting up of the Messiah on the cross looks like weakness, but from heaven's vantage point, the cross is a demonstration of divine power, strength, and wisdom (see 1 Cor 1:18–25). As stated earlier, all these events are now fulfilling God's ancient promises to his people. An example of one of God's Davidic promises being fulfilled in Christ can be found in 2 Samuel:

> "The LORD declares to you: The LORD himself will make a house for you. When your time comes and you rest with your ancestors, I will raise up after you your descendant, who will come from your body, and I will establish his kingdom. He is the one who will build a house for my name, and I will establish the throne of his kingdom forever . . . so that your name will be exalted forever, when it is said, 'The LORD of Armies is God over Israel.'" (2 Sam 7:11–13, 26)

Another example of the fulfillment of an ancient Davidic promise is found in the book of Amos:

> In that day
> I will restore the fallen shelter of David:
> I will repair its gaps,
> restore its ruins,

---

[10] Like Matthew, Luke highlights Jesus's Davidic origin throughout his Birth and Infancy narrative (Luke 1:27, 32; 2:4, 11).

and rebuild it as in the days of old, so that they may
> possess
the remnant of Edom
and all the nations
that bear my name—
this is the declaration of the LORD; he will do this.
> (Amos 9:11–12)

What God said he would do in the distant past, he was now
bringing to fulfillment in Christ.

Zechariah's words, "Salvation from our enemies and from
the hand of all who hate us" (v. 71), likely were thought by
Zechariah to refer to deliverance from Roman occupation.[11]
For Luke's readers, however, they understood his words to be
God's deliverance of his people from their spiritual enemies—
Satan, sin, and death. Jesus brought spiritual deliverance as the
divine Messiah.

Fulfillment of God's Promises to Abraham (1:72–75)

Zechariah goes on to declare how God's great mercy is being
demonstrated in the fulfillment of God's covenant to Israel,
especially the Abrahamic covenant (vv. 72–73).

"By myself I have sworn," this is the LORD's declaration:
"Because you have done this thing and have not with-
held your only son, I will indeed bless you and make

---

[11] David E. Garland, *Luke*, Zondervan Exegetical Commentary on the
New Testament (Grand Rapids: Zondervan, 2011), 107. Garland understands Zechariah's language of salvation to mean that Israel will be able to
serve God without persecution from her enemies.

your offspring as numerous as the stars of the sky and the sand on the seashore. Your offspring will possess the city gates of their enemies. And all the nations of the earth will be blessed by your offspring because you have obeyed my command." (Gen 22:16–18)

God's covenant with Abraham was the foundation of Israel's self-understanding as God's special people. God's oath to Abraham focused on Abraham's descendants and on the possession of the land of Canaan (Gen 22:16–18; Ps 105:8–11). The covenant with Abraham included the blessing of all nations through Abraham's descendants (Gen 12:3; 22:18). While the theme of blessing to all nations is not highlighted in this passage, it is a key feature in Simeon's *Nunc Dimittis* (Luke 2:31–32). One thing Zechariah makes abundantly clear is that God keeps his promises, every one of them. Micah 7:20 captures this idea.

You will show loyalty to Jacob and faithful love to Abraham, as you swore to our ancestors from days long ago.

The goal of God's deliverance of his people from spiritual captivity is their freedom to serve him without fear (vv. 74–75).[12] When God's people understand everything God has done for them in Christ, they demonstrate their love for him by serving him in righteousness and holiness for his glory. Those who grasp the true meaning of Christmas feel compelled to serve God by serving his people. Many in the church today need to reread Zechariah's words; life is not about being served but about serving God's people for God's glory.

---

[12] Bock, *Luke*, 1:185–86.

Zechariah's Words Concerning John (1:76–80)

After briefly tracing God's promises and works throughout
redemptive history, Zechariah turns his attention to his son, John
(v. 76). Zechariah focuses on John's role in the unfolding drama
of redemption. John will be recognized as a divinely empowered
prophet. His prophetic role involves preparing the way—but for
whom? John's connection with Elijah suggests he is preparing
the way for Yahweh's coming (cf. Luke 1:17). Indeed, this is made
clear by the reference to preparing the way for the Lord (v. 76).
While Zechariah clearly thought the reference was directed
towards Yahweh, Luke's readers understood the reference to be
directed toward the coming of Jesus as God's incarnate Son. God
visited his people in the person of his Son.[13]

The salvation of which Zechariah has been speaking is identified here as "the knowledge of salvation" and "the forgiveness of
sins" (v. 77). The terms salvation and forgiveness are important
terms for Luke.[14] The thematic verse for Luke's Gospel may very
well be 19:10, "For the Son of Man has come to seek and to save
the lost." The apostle Paul stated the matter this way, "'Christ
Jesus came into the world to save sinners'—and I am the worst
of them" (1 Tim 1:15). Forgiveness of sin is an integral part of
the new covenant set forth in Jeremiah, "For I will forgive their
iniquity and never again remember their sin" (Jer 31:34).

Forgiveness of sin would have meant much to a Gentile like
Luke. Paul expressed the desperate condition of the Gentiles in
Eph 2:11–12, "So, then, remember that at one time you were

---

[13] Stein, *Luke*, 1:101.

[14] On the thought of salvation in Luke's Gospel, see "Taking a Deeper
Dive" at the conclusion of this chapter.

Gentiles in the flesh—called 'the uncircumcised' by those called 'the circumcised,' which is done in the flesh by human hands. At that time, you were without Christ, excluded from the citizenship of Israel, and foreigners to the covenants of promise, without hope and without God in the world." While the old covenant excluded Gentiles, the new covenant promises forgiveness of sin for all who are in Christ.

This promise of forgiveness in Zechariah's song is played out in Luke's Gospel. For example, John the Baptist connected the importance of repentance and forgiveness in his preaching to the crowds (3:3). Jesus forgave the sins of a paralytic (5:20) and a woman with a bad reputation (7:47–48). In his final instructions to his disciples, Jesus told them to preach "forgiveness of sins" to all nations (24:47). In the Lord's prayer, Jesus instructed his disciples to ask for God's forgiveness for their sin and forgive those who have sinned against them (11:4). Jesus did exactly this when he prayed, "Father, forgive them, because they do not know what they are doing" (23:34). In the book of Acts, Stephen followed Jesus's example when he prayed for those who were stoning him (7:60). We do not know for certain what kind of impact Stephen's words made on Saul of Tarsus (7:58), but Paul expressed the same forgiveness at the end of his life when commenting about those who deserted him, "May it not be counted against them" (2 Tim 4:16). Bitterness and resentment are not options for the child of God.

Christ's coming is an expression of God's great compassionate mercy (v. 78a). The mercy is described by comparing the Messiah's coming to a beautiful sunrise that dispels the darkness (v. 78b).[15] The phrase "the dawn from on high" is translated

---

[15] For more on v. 78, see Bock, *Luke*, 1:491–9; Garland, *Luke*, 168–70; Stein, *Luke*, 180.

in the KJV, "the dayspring [*anatolē*] from on high hath visited
us." The KJV translation leads some to interpret "dayspring"
as a messianic title. The NASB translation reads, "the Sunrise
[*anatolē*] from on high will visit us." The Greek word *anatolē* is
used in the Septuagint to translate the messianic title "branch" in
Jer 23:5 and Zech 3:8; 6:12.[16] But the word itself literally means
"the rising" and ordinarily refers to sunrise. The imagery in v. 78
speaks to the coming of light into the world, a light that descends
from heaven and drives out the world's darkness. Zechariah does
not link this imagery specifically to Jesus, but Luke's readers certainly understood God's coming into the world through Christ
to be the beginning of the dispelling of the spiritual darkness
of sin and death, much like the sunrise gradually eliminates the
night's darkness.[17]

The thought concerning light continues in the next verse,
where Zechariah alludes to Isaiah 9 (Luke 1:79): "The people
walking in darkness have seen a great light; a light has dawned
on those living in the land of darkness" (Isa 9:2). Isaiah 9:1–7 is
a messianic prophecy speaking of the child to be born who will
reign on David's throne. One title ascribed to this child in the
Isaiah passage is "Mighty God" (Isa 9:6), and he will lead God's
people into "the way of peace," meaning peace with God (v. 79;
cf. Rom 5:1–2).

The passage concludes with a reference to John living in the
wilderness (v. 80). This is likely a reference to the uninhabited
area near the Jordan River. The "wilderness" was often used as an
image of Israel's hopes of a new beginning and the place where

---

[16] See the discussion in Bock, *Luke*, 1:192.

[17] On the imagery of light in the Bible and particularly as it relates to
the incarnation, see "Taking a Deeper Dive," chapter 1.

they grew in their knowledge of God (cf. Isa 40:3; Jer 2:2–3). We do not know John's age when he began to live in the wilderness. Although his parents were elderly, we do not know when they died. Furthermore, we do not know what, if any, interaction John may have had with others during his wilderness years. Did he interact with the Essenes at Qumran? Again, we simply do not know. What we do know is that God was preparing him for a brief but powerful ministry.

Final Reflections

While this passage has much to say to every believer, the focus will be on two main points. First, Zechariah's reference to the term "covenant" is found nowhere else in the Gospels except in Jesus's words at the Last Supper (v. 72; cf., Matt 26:28; Mark 14:24; Luke 22:20). Jesus spoke to his disciples in the upper room about the beginning of a new covenant. God's plan of salvation can be traced from Abraham through David and all the way to Christ. God's purposes had been consistent from days of old, until the unfolding of the events in Christ. As God's Messiah, Jesus's ministry would be a blessing to all the nations of the world. As a result of Christ's work, God's people are redeemed from Satan, sin, and death; and they will serve him in righteousness and holiness for his glory. God's people will have the knowledge of salvation, experience the forgiveness of sin, and rejoice that they are no longer living in darkness but are light in the Lord. All of these are the blessings of peace. Such a comprehensive understanding of God's purposes in human history opens the door for a greater trust in God's providence in our lives today. God's covenant promises have indeed come to fulfillment in Jesus Christ.

Second, Zechariah and Elizabeth remained immovable on naming their baby John, the name given by Gabriel. While this seems like a small matter, it is much larger than one would anticipate. By naming the baby John, they went against cultural tradition and family expectations. The couple's commitment to God mattered more than what others might think of their decision. Zechariah had clearly learned the consequences of disobedience.

A Christmas Hymn of Response

While by the sheep we watched at night,
Glad tidings brought an angel bright.
How great our joy! Great our joy!
Joy, joy, joy! Joy, joy, joy!
Praise we the Lord in heav'n on high!
Praise we the Lord in heav'n on high!

There shall be born, so he did say,
In Bethlehem a Child today.
How great our joy! Great our joy!
Joy, joy, joy! Joy, joy, joy!
Praise we the Lord in heav'n on high!
Praise we the Lord in heav'n on high!

There shall the Child lie in a stall,
This Child who shall redeem us all.
How great our joy! Great our joy!
Joy, joy, joy! Joy, joy, joy!
Praise we the Lord in heav'n on high!
Praise we the Lord in heav'n on high!

This gift of God we'll cherish well,

That ever joy our hearts shall fill.

How great our joy! Great our joy!

Joy, joy, joy! Joy, joy, joy!

Praise we the Lord in heav'n on high!

Praise we the Lord in heav'n on high![18]

Taking a Deeper Dive: Salvation in Luke's Gospel

Three of the four uses of the noun "salvation" in Luke's Gospel appear in Zechariah's *Benedictus* (1:69, 71, 77). The word is used only once in Mark's and John's Gospels and never in Matthew's. The verb "to save" (*sōzō*) is used frequently in Luke (fifteen times). The salvation Jesus provides is for all people, especially those on the fringes of Jewish society. Jesus told an unnamed immoral woman, "Your faith has saved you" (7:50). Those with hard hearts who hear God's word are in grave danger of the devil snatching the word "so that they may not believe and be saved" (8:12). In Luke 8:36, the crowd reported how the demon-possessed Gadarene was *healed* (*sōzō*). The man was not only set free but converted, that is, saved. The dramatic change, because of the man's encounter with Jesus, clearly communicates that something more than mental and emotional healing has taken place in his life.

The scope of those who are saved is astonishing. For example, when Luke applies Isa 40:3 to John the Baptist, he is the only Gospel writer to extend the quotation to Isa 40:5: "and everyone will see the salvation of God" (3:6). Those words must have meant much to Luke and his Gentile readers. When asked

---

[18] Author Unknown, "How Great Our Joy," date unknown, *Baptist Hymnal*, #108.

why he ate with tax collectors and sinners, Jesus responded with the parables of the lost sheep, the lost coin, and the lost son (15:1–32). When one sinner is saved, there is rejoicing in heaven. God will not be satisfied until his banquet hall is filled (14:24). Those who Jesus, the great physician, saves are not the self-righteous (Pharisees) but the sick (tax collectors and sinners) (5:31). Jesus has come to save sinners as the following verses indicate (italics added).

- When Simon Peter saw this, he fell at Jesus's knees and said, "Go away from me, because I'm a *sinful* man, Lord." (5:8)
- But the Pharisees and their scribes were complaining to his disciples, "Why do you eat and drink with *tax collectors and sinners*?" (5:30)
- "I have not come to call the righteous, but *sinners* to repentance." (5:32)
- "The Son of Man has come eating and drinking, and you say, 'Look, a glutton and a drunkard, a friend of *tax collectors and sinners*!'" (7:34)
- And a woman in the town who was a *sinner* found out that Jesus was reclining at the table in the Pharisee's house. She brought an alabaster jar of perfume and stood behind him at his feet, weeping, and began to wash his feet with her tears. She wiped his feet with her hair, kissing them and anointing them with the perfume. (7:37–38)
- And the Pharisees and scribes were complaining, "This man welcomes *sinners* and eats with them." (15:2)
- "I tell you, in the same way, there will be more joy in heaven over one *sinner* who repents than over ninety-nine

righteous people who don't need repentance." (15:7, cf. v. 10)

- But the *tax collector*, standing far off, would not even raise his eyes to heaven but kept striking his chest and saying, "God, have mercy on me, a sinner!" (18:13)
- All who saw it began to complain, "He's gone to stay with a *sinful* man." (19:7)

Clearly, Jesus came into the world to save sinners. The importance of Jesus's coming to redeem sinners is often a forgotten message of Christmas. Amidst the hustle and bustle of the season, many forget the true message of the holiday. Jesus left heaven's throne for Bethlehem's manger to die on a cross and be raised on the third day. The birth in Bethlehem's manger must lead to a cross on Golgotha's hill. The better we understand this purpose of Jesus's coming, the more seriously we will take our responsibility to evangelize those Jesus came to save.

Zechariah's comparison of the coming of the Messiah to the rising of the sun reveals the glorious nature of Jesus's coming and the desperate situation of those he came to save. Outside of Christ, people are in spiritual darkness. Paul stated, "The god of this age has blinded the minds of the unbelievers to keep them from seeing the light of the gospel of the glory of Christ, who is the image of God" (2 Cor 4:4). The coming of the Messiah brought the light of the gospel that allows people to begin to see their need for a Savior. Salvation means God has rescued us from "the domain of darkness and transferred us into the kingdom of the Son he loves" (Col 1:13). The birth of King Jesus meant "the people walking in darkness have seen a great light; a light has dawned on those living in the land of darkness" (Isa 9:2). Praise be to God for the coming of the Light of the World!

CHAPTER 7

THE ANNUNCIATION
TO JOSEPH

MATTHEW 1:18–25

> "She will give birth to a son, and you
> are to name him Jesus, because he will
> save his people from their sins."
> —Matthew 1:21

Compared to Luke's birth announcements to Zechariah and Mary, Matthew's annunciation seems straightforward and unadorned. Yet the Gospel of Matthew recounts the terrible dilemma Joseph suddenly found himself in—betrothed to a pregnant woman and the baby was not his child. This is the kind of small-town scandal that would rock an entire community. A young lady with a pristine reputation is discovered to be pregnant, and her betrothed husband is not the child's father. We do not know for certain when Joseph became aware of Mary's pregnancy, but we do know the news must have caused him unspeakable sorrow. Adultery is one of the greatest betrayals a person can experience. While Joseph's brokenheartedness is not mentioned, we can only imagine the thoughts that raced through his mind when he learned of the news. The passage unfolds in a straightforward manner: Joseph's dreadful dilemma (vv. 18–19), Joseph's dramatic encounter with Gabriel (vv. 20–23), and Joseph's prompt obedience (vv. 24–25).

A Shocking Scandal (1:18–19)

Joseph is depicted as a man of impeccable character (*dikaios*) and tremendous compassion. Surely these were two qualities God the Father looked for in a man to raise his Son. The qualities of righteousness and compassion are not always found together. On the one hand, some people of firm convictions find empathizing with people who do not live up to their standards difficult. On the other hand, some people's compassion leads them to overlook the sinful choices of others. Joseph embodied both qualities—conviction and compassion. In many ways, Joseph is one of the unsung heroes (along with Simeon and Anna) of the Christmas story.

Matthew begins his description of the events with Joseph's decision to divorce Mary. While Matthew states, "The birth of Jesus came about this way," he does not actually describe the birth itself or the events surrounding Jesus's birth. The word translated "birth" in v. 18 is the same word (*genesis*) translated "beginning" in Matt 1:1. For Matthew, the story begins with Joseph's dilemma (v. 18). Matthew's words, "She [Mary] was found to be with child," should not be interpreted to mean that they had tried to keep her pregnancy secret, but the simple fact that her pregnancy was made known.[1] Matthew immediately makes clear

---

[1] D. A. Carson, "Matthew," in *Matthew and Mark*, ed. Tremper Longman III and David E. Garland, The Expositor's Bible Commentary (Grand Rapids: Zondervan, 2010), 74.

to the reader that Mary's pregnancy was the result of the power-ful working of the Holy Spirit; however, Joseph initially would not have been aware of this fact. The phrase "before they came together" means before they had sexual relations. Luke, and now Matthew, both affirm Mary's virginal conception of Jesus.

As mentioned above, Joseph unexpectedly finds himself in an untenable situation. Although referred to as Mary's husband, the betrothal process had not yet been consummated by their sexual union. As mentioned earlier, the betrothal process took place in several steps.[2] Typically, the process was initiated by the parents of the young man choosing the young lady to be engaged to their son. The next step in the process was a formal prenuptial agreement between the two families. At this point, the couple were considered betrothed to one another. The young man and young lady were considered husband and wife at this point, but the couple would not sexually consummate the marriage yet. The young woman continued to live in her parents' home. Sexual infi-delity would be considered adultery and grounds for divorce. In addition, if one of the parties died during this period, the other would be considered a widow or widower. Approximately one year after entering into the formal agreement, the official wed-ding ceremony took place. The couple consummated the mar-riage sexually at that time. Wedding festivities could last up to one week.

We should not assume Joseph and Mary had a twenty-first-century romantic kind of love for one another when the pro-cess began. However, they likely knew each other, unlike some arranged marriages, since they lived in a small village. While

---

[2] Michael J. Wilkins, *Matthew*, Zondervan Illustrated Bible Back-grounds Commentary (Grand Rapids: Zondervan, 2002), 11.

their interactions would have been limited over the years, their families decided the couple should marry, have children, and spend their lives together. Even in that culture, there would have been an increasing anticipation of marital union.

Joseph's determination to divorce (*apolyō*) Mary quietly demonstrated a graciousness on his part and reflected an aspect of his character that becomes even clearer as the story unfolds. Nevertheless, scandal loomed on the horizon. Although adultery was a serious sin, execution for adultery was seldom practiced at this time.[3] Even if Mary explained the circumstances to Joseph, believing that Mary became pregnant without sexual union with a man would be difficult, if not impossible, for him to believe.[4] As a righteous man, Joseph had no choice but to divorce her. Deuteronomy 24:1 says, "If a man marries a woman, but she becomes displeasing to him because he finds something indecent about her, he may write her a divorce certificate, hand it to her, and send her away from his house." Rabbis of the day debated what was meant by the words "something indecent" (Matt 19:1–10).[5] The followers of Rabbi Hillel interpreted the words to mean that a man could divorce his wife for almost any reason, even if he no longer found her attractive. The followers of Rabbi Shammai believed that a man could divorce his wife only if she had been unfaithful to him. If a man sought to divorce his wife, he needed only to write a document stating that his wife

---

[3] Craig S. Keener, *A Commentary on the Gospel of Matthew* (Grand Rapids: Zondervan, 2002), 91.

[4] Keener, *Matthew*, 92, suggests that in first century Jewish culture the couple would not have had much time alone nor have gotten many opportunities to get to know one another well. Therefore, there was little reason for Joseph to believe Mary.

[5] Wilkins, *Matthew*, ZIBC, 117.

was free from him and could remarry.[6] No civil action, such as going before a court, was necessary.

A Message from Heaven (1:20–23)

At this point, Joseph is visited by an angel in a dream (v. 20). This is the first of several dreams providing Joseph providential direction (Matt 2:12, 13, 19, 22; cf. 27:19). The Jewish people believed God communicated his will through dreams. For example, Num 12:6 says, "Listen to what I say: If there is a prophet among you from the Lord, I make myself known to him in a vision; I speak with him in a dream."

The angel's message to Joseph came in "the nick of time" and convinced Joseph of Mary's innocence. While Joseph may not have understood the full significance of the announcement, Matthew's readers certainly did.[7] The angel addressed Joseph as a "son of David." This is the only time in Matthew's Gospel that someone other than Jesus is identified by the title. Scholars debate whether Mary was also a descendant of David or if Jesus's Davidic lineage came through Joseph as his adoptive father. What can be said is that Mary is never specifically identified as a descendant of David. The name "Jesus" (*Iēsous*) is used three times in this passage, highlighting its significance (vv. 21, 23, 25). In fact, the final word in the passage is "Jesus," indicating Joseph's obedience to the angel's command to name the child Jesus. The angel associates Jesus's name with his mission. As mentioned earlier, the name Jesus means "Yahweh saves." Jesus's mission is to "save his people from their sins" (*hamartia*) (v. 21).

---

[6] Wilkins, *Matthew*, ZIBC, 117.

[7] On the historicity of the virgin birth, see Carson, "Matthew," 95–99.

Matthew then informs his readers (vv. 22–23) that these things took place to fulfill Isa 7:14. This is the first of several Old Testament references intended to show that Jesus's life fulfilled the Hebrew Scriptures. Many of these references are introduced by the phrase "all this took place to fulfill what had been spoken by the Lord through the prophet." Below are a few examples found in Matthew (italics added).

> *Now all this took place to fulfill* what was spoken by the Lord through the prophet: See, the virgin will become pregnant and give birth to a son, and they will name him Immanuel. (1:22–23)

> In Bethlehem of Judea," they told him, "because *this is what was written by the prophet*: And you, Bethlehem, in the land of Judah, are by no means least among the rulers of Judah: Because out of you will come a ruler who will shepherd my people Israel." (2:5–6)

> He stayed there until Herod's death, so that what was *spoken by the Lord through the prophet* might be fulfilled: Out of Egypt I called my Son. (2:15)

> Then *what was spoken through Jeremiah the prophet* was fulfilled: A voice was heard in Ramah, weeping, and great mourning, Rachel weeping for her children; and she refused to be consoled, because they are no more. (2:17–18)

> Then he [Joseph] went and settled in a town called Nazareth to fulfill what was spoken through the prophets, that he would be called a Nazarene. (2:23)

How Matthew uses Isa 7:14 is debated. Before examining the various interpretive approaches, we begin with the historical context of Isaiah 7. The Kings of Syria and Israel plotted to go to war against Ahaz, king of Judah. Ahaz was a Davidic descendant; thus, the war was an assault on the house of David. The prophet Isaiah told Ahaz that the plot against him and his house would not take place. God encouraged Ahaz to ask for a sign of confirmation, but Ahaz refused, saying that he did not want to test the Lord. Then Isaiah said: "Therefore, the LORD himself will give you a sign: See, the virgin will conceive, have a son, and name him Immanuel. By the time he learns to reject what is bad and choose what is good, he will be eating curds and honey. For before the boy knows to reject what is bad and choose what is good, the land of the two kings you dread will be abandoned" (Isa 7:14–16).

From all appearances, Isaiah spoke about a child to be born during Ahaz's lifetime. The child would be alive when the kings of Syria and Israel failed to take the Southern Kingdom. The angel's quotation of the prophecy to Joseph suggests (in some sense) Jesus fulfilled the prophecy. This is one of many places in Matthew's Gospel where he cites an Old Testament passage that appears to be about something or someone other than Jesus, and then Matthew proceeds to say that Jesus fulfilled the prophecy.

Bible scholars have long debated how Matthew understood the Isaiah passage. One issue is how Matthew understood the term translated "virgin." The Hebrew term in Isaiah for virgin is *almah*, which is not the technical term for virgin (*bethula*). The Septuagint, however, translates *almah* with the Greek word *parthenos* (the same word used in Matt 1:23 where Isa 7:14 is quoted), and *parthenos* means "virgin." The Septuagint translators of Isa 7:14 would likely not have used *parthenos* if they did not understand Isaiah to be referring to a virgin.

The second issue centers on Matthew's use of Isa 7:14. The following is a summary of a longer discussion by David Turner on the three most common interpretations of Matthew's use of Isa 7:14.[8] The first interpretation is the predictive approach. Those who hold to the predictive approach understand Matthew's use of Isa 7:14 as a direct prophecy fulfilled in the virginal conception of Jesus. Therefore, the prophecy goes beyond the contemporary circumstances in Ahaz's day and is a sign pointing to Jesus's day. In this interpretation, the sign really has no significant meaning for Ahaz.[9] Those who hold to this view contend that only the predictive view does justice to the sign's name being "Immanuel" ("God is with us"). The strength of this position is the clear focus on the New Testament fulfillment of the Old Testament prophecy. Those who hold this direct fulfillment approach argue that the birth of a son would provide little assurance to Ahaz that the invasion would be averted.

The second approach to the interpretation of Isa 7:14 is the typological view. This understanding points to the historical context. Therefore, Isa 7:14 is understood to be a sign fulfilled during Ahaz's day. When Isaiah made his prophecy, the woman who eventually gave birth to the child was a virgin. However, her conception of the child would be through the sexual relations between a man and a woman. If this interpretation is correct, then Matthew understands the Isaiah passage as a historical pattern that comes to ultimate fulfillment with the birth of Jesus. A young woman in Isaiah's day conceived a child who served as a sign of deliverance to Ahaz and the house of

---

[8] See David L. Turner, *The Gospel of Matthew: Tyndale Cornerstone Biblical Commentary*, vol. 11 (Carol Stream, IL: Tyndale House, 2005), 42–45.

[9] Carson, "Matthew," 78–79.

David (Isa 7:2, 13). But more importantly, a young woman in Matthew's day who was literally a virgin, conceived a child by the Spirit. This child was from the line of David. In Isaiah's day, the child was a sign of God's presence and help in the deliverance of Ahaz. In Matthew's day, the child was himself "God is with us," the ultimate deliverer.[10] The strength of this interpretation is that the original prophecy had historical significance for the original setting, as well as finding ultimate fulfillment in Matthew's day.

The third approach is the multiple fulfillment view. This approach to Isa 7:14 understands there to have been a partial fulfillment in Ahaz's day, but a greater and more climactic fulfillment in Jesus.[11] The prophet Isaiah may not have fully understood this, but Isaiah was merely the messenger. The prophecy ultimately came from God. Therefore, the prophecy from the divine author (God) was not fully understood by the human prophet. The strength of this position is that both the original prophecy and Matthew's use of the prophecy are relevant.

Turner suggests that one should be hesitant to be too dogmatic on this matter since significant scholars can be found advocating each view.[12] Whichever approach is taken in the interpretation of Isa 7:14, each interpretation arrives at the same conclusion—Jesus is "Immanuel." I find the typological view most convincing for the reasons stated above. Matthew will use the typological approach again in his Birth and Infancy narrative.

---

[10] Michael F. Bird, *Jesus Is the Christ* (Downers Grove: InterVarsity, 2012), 64.

[11] Craig L. Blomberg, *Matthew*, vol. 22, The New American Commentary (Nashville: Holman Reference, 1992), 59–60.

[12] Turner, *The Gospel of Matthew*, 43.

Joseph: A Man of Prompt Obedience (1:24–25)

Just as Mary willingly and immediately embraced God's will in response to the angel's words, Joseph did the same. After waking from his dream, Joseph took Mary as his wife. The one thing he did not do was consummate the marriage by sexual union until after Jesus's birth. This abstinence ensured that Jesus was not his biological child. In contrast to the growing acceptance of casual sex outside of marriage in our day, Joseph demonstrated himself to be a man of great self-control. Again, another quality that God the Father would surely want in the man to raise his Son.

Final Reflections

As the story continues to unfold, we see God using holy people in the accomplishment of his will. The people God brought onto the stage of redemptive history had been in his divine workshop for most of their lives. God had been crafting them into useful instruments fit for his service. Joseph was one of those individuals. Joseph's role in this dramatic drama is often overlooked. We don't know much about him, but what we do know epitomizes his godly character. The description of his actions in Matthew 1 and 2 and Luke 2:21–23 establishes him as being deeply committed to God. While God is obviously free to use whomever he chooses in the accomplishment of his will, he primarily chooses those wholly devoted to him.

A second thought to reflect on is the meaning of Jesus's name, "God is with us" (Immanuel).[13] This idea will reappear in the final words of the Great Commission, "And remember, I am

---

[13] For a fuller discussion on Christ's deity see "Taking a Deeper Dive" at the conclusion of this chapter.

with you always, to the end of the age" (Matt 28:20). The celebration of Christ's coming reminds his people that we are never alone. Although we may feel betrayed, abandoned, and isolated, Jesus, Immanuel, is always with us. As the psalmist wrote,

> Where can I go to escape your Spirit?
> Where can I flee from your presence?
> If I go up to heaven, you are there;
> if I make my bed in Sheol, you are there.
> If I fly on the wings of the dawn
> and settle down on the western horizon,
> even there your hand will lead me;
> your right hand will hold on to me.
> If I say, "Surely the darkness will hide me,
> And the light around me will be night"—
> even the darkness is not dark to you.
> The night shines like the day;
> darkness and light are alike to you. (Ps 139:7–12)

"God with us" means we are never alone. Even when we are abandoned by loved ones and friends, God is with us!

A Christmas Hymn of Response

> Angels, from the realms of glory,
> Wing your flight o'er all the earth;
> Ye who sang creation's story,
> Now proclaim Messiah's birth:
> Come and worship, come and worship,
> Worship Christ, the newborn King!
>
> Shepherds, in the fields abiding,
> Watching o'er your flocks by night,
> God with man is now residing,

Yonder shines the infant Light:
Come and worship, come and worship,
Worship Christ, the newborn King!

Sages, leave your contemplations,
Brighter visions beam afar;
Seek the great Desire of nations,
Ye have seen the Infant's star:
Come and worship, come and worship,
Worship Christ, the newborn King!

Saints before the altar bending,
Watching long in hope and fear,
Suddenly the Lord, descending,
In His temple shall appear:
Come and worship, come and worship,
Worship Christ, the newborn King![14]

Taking a Deeper Dive: Jesus Is "*God* with Us"

The church's conviction that Jesus Christ is God is called into question by skeptics. Many understand the belief in Jesus's divinity to be no different than a child's belief in Santa Claus. Just as children outgrow a belief in Santa Claus, so one must cast aside a belief in Jesus's deity when one reaches adulthood. Others make the statement that Jesus never claimed to be God, but later generations of his followers elevated him to the status of deity.[15] Some

---

[14] James Montgomery, "Angels from the Realms of Glory," 1962, *The Baptist Hymnal*, #94.

[15] For two discussions denying the deity of Jesus, see Bart D. Ehrman, *How Jesus Became God: The Exaltation of a Jewish Preacher from Galilee*

liberal scholars affirm Jesus to have been a great moral teacher but maintain that he clearly was not God and nor did he ever claim to be. Some liberal scholarship often suggests the Jesus of history became the Christ of faith. In other words, the church's understanding of the identity of Jesus evolved over the centuries. While my intention is not to make a scholarly defense of Christ's divinity here (others have done that), I do intend to show that the Bible clearly teaches the deity of Christ. For evangelical Christians, the Bible is the foundation for faith and practice and is a sufficient guide for understanding this essential doctrine.

As mentioned above, some claim that Jesus never declared himself to be God. Yet, in one of Jesus's most straightforward statements concerning who he believed himself to be, his adversaries understood him to be confessing equality with God. The religious leadership made the slanderous statement that Jesus was a Samaritan and demon-possessed (John 8:48), a claim Jesus forthrightly rejected. In response, he declared, "Truly I tell you, before Abraham was, I am *(egō eimi)*" (John 8:58). Jewish Christians would think immediately of Exod 3:14, where God revealed himself to Moses in the burning bush. God disclosed his personal name to Moses in the dramatic encounter as Yahweh ("I am"). Jesus made abundantly clear to his opponents that he believed himself to be the one who

---

(San Francisco: Harper One, 2014), and Marcus Borg in Marcus J. Borg and N. T. Wright, *The Meaning of Jesus: Two Visions* (San Francisco: HarperCollins, 1999), 146–68. Wright argues against Borg in this chapter. For a defense of Jesus's deity, see John Stott, *Basic Christianity*, 50th anniversary ed. (Downers Grove: IVP, 2008), 29–74. My approach here follows Stott's. For a rebuttal of Ehrman see Michael F. Bird et al., *How God Became Jesus: The Real Origins of Belief in Jesus' Divine Nature—A Response to Bart Ehrman* (Grand Rapids: Zondervan, 2014).

spoke to Moses from the burning bush. In other words, Jesus believed himself to be God. The religious leaders knew exactly what Jesus was claiming for himself. As a result, they picked up stones to kill him.

During the Feast of Hanukkah, Jesus told the Jewish leadership, "I and the Father are one" (John 10:30). Again, they understood the gravity of his shocking pronouncement and attempted to stone him. When Jesus asked them why they wanted to stone him, they replied, "We aren't stoning you for a good work . . . but for blasphemy, because you—being a man—make yourself God" (John 10:33). To the religious leaders of Jesus's day, his claims to equality with God were unmistakable.

To these explicit claims of equality with God by Jesus, we can add several implicit claims by Jesus to deity. Jesus said, "I am the bread of life . . . No one who comes to me will ever be hungry, and no one who believes in me will ever be thirsty again" (John 6:35). "I am the light of the world. Anyone who follows me will never walk in the darkness but will have the light of life" (John 8:12). "I am the resurrection and the life. The one who believes in me, even if he dies, will live. Everyone who lives and believes in me will never die" (John 11:25–26). "I am the way, the truth, and the life. No one comes to the Father except through me" (John 14:6). These claims by Jesus are astonishing. Those who believe in him will never be spiritually hungry or thirsty. Those who follow him will never walk in spiritual darkness. Those who trust in him will live even if they die. According to Jesus, the only way one can have a relationship with God is through him (John 14:6). To paraphrase C. S. Lewis, these claims could only be made by a liar (he knew he wasn't God), a lunatic (he thought he was God in a delusional manner), or he was God in human flesh. Those who deny Jesus claimed to be God must deny the historical veracity of the biblical record.

Is there other evidence in the Bible affirming Jesus's deity? As noted earlier, in John's prologue, we read that "all things were created through him, and apart from him not one thing was created that has been created" (John 1:3). The opening and closing verses of John's prologue indisputably declare that Jesus Christ is God: "In the beginning was the Word, and the Word was with God, and the Word was God. . . . No one has ever seen God. The one and only Son, who is himself God and is at the Father's side—he has revealed him" (John 1:1, 18). In Paul's epistle to the Colossians, he stated that all things were created through Jesus, that all things were created for him and he upholds and maintains his creation (Col 1:16–17).

In addition to these assertions of Christ's divinity, we turn to his works. If we believe that the Scriptures accurately record Jesus's deeds, then many of his miracles attest to his deity. In other words, Jesus did what no ordinary human being could do.[16] For example, Jesus turned approximately 175 gallons of water into wine (John 2:1–11). He healed a dying boy from approximately sixteen miles away (John 4:46–54). Jesus healed a crippled man

---

[16] Graham Twelftree is one of the leading authorities on the miracles and exorcisms of Jesus. He argues in several works that the evidence that Jesus was a miracle-worker is so strong it is one of the best-attested historical facts about Jesus. See Graham Twelftree, "The History of Miracles in the History of Jesus," in *New Testament Studies: A Survey of Recent Research*, ed. Scot McKnight and Grant R. Osborne (Grand Rapids: Baker Academic, 2004). Twelftree writes, "There is now almost unanimous agreement among Jesus's questers that the historical Jesus performed mighty works" (206). On the historical reliability of John's Gospel see Craig L. Blomberg, *The Historical Reliability of John's Gospel* (Downers Grove: InterVarsity, 2001).

who had not walked in thirty-eight years (John 5:1–16). In the
ensuing discussion, the Jewish leaders understood Jesus's actions
and comments to be a claim to equality with God (John 5:17–
18). Jesus fed thousands of people with a few pieces of bread and
a couple of fish (John 6:1–15). Jesus walked on the Sea of Galilee
(John 6:16–21). Later in his ministry, Jesus healed a man born
blind by smearing mud on his eyes and having him wash the mud
off in the pool of Siloam (John 9:6–7). The culminating miracle
performed by Jesus in the Fourth Gospel is the resurrection of
Lazarus (John 11:43–44). One may argue over the historicity
of these events, but if these miracles are found to be historically
credible, they most certainly attest that Jesus Christ did what no
ordinary human being could possibly do, and they thereby signal
his deity. While one may reject the deity of Jesus, they cannot
deny the Bible teaches it. Many more verses could be included,
but these should be sufficient to establish that the Bible teaches
the deity of Christ.[17]

Why give so much consideration to Jesus's deity? When
Gabriel said the baby is to be called "Immanuel," Jesus truly is
"God with us." Therefore, when he told his disciples in the final
words of Matthew's Gospel, "And remember, I am with you
always, to the end of the age," Jesus truly meant it. The incarnation is about God taking on human flesh and becoming one of
us. J. I. Packer wrote, "God became man; the divine son became a
human; the Almighty appeared on the earth as a helpless human
baby, unable to do more than live and stare and wriggle and make
noises, needing to be fed and changed and taught to talk like

---

[17] For an accessible exposition of John's Gospel, see William F. Cook,
John: Jesus Christ Is God, Focus on the Bible (Scotland, UK: Christian
Focus, 2016).

any other child . . . Nothing in fiction is so fantastic as is this truth of the Incarnation."[18] The apostle Paul stated beautifully in Phil 2:6–8 that Jesus is the one

> who, existing in the form of God,
> did not consider equality with God
> as something to be exploited.
> Instead he emptied himself
> by assuming the form of a servant,
> taking on the likeness of humanity.
> And when he had come as a man,
> he humbled himself by becoming obedient to the point
>   of death—
> even to death on a cross.

At so many points in the Birth and Infancy narratives, one is faced with a moment of decision. Is Jesus Christ who the Bible says he is? Is Jesus God? To affirm Jesus's divinity is to say the one thing contemporary culture says you cannot say. The moment you confess that Jesus Christ is God, you imply that what Jesus says is true. If what Jesus said is true, then there is no other way a person can be made right with God except through Jesus. If Jesus is God, then he is our Creator and deserves our loving devotion and faithful obedience. Considering what the Bible teaches about Jesus, the ultimate question is: "Who do you believe Jesus Christ to be?"

---

[18] J. I. Packer, *Knowing God* (Downers Grove: InterVarsity, 1975), 53.

CHAPTER 8

THE BIRTH OF JESUS

LUKE 2:1–7

> "Then she gave birth to her firstborn son,
> and she wrapped him tightly in cloth and
> laid him in a manger, because there was
> no guest room available for them."
> —Luke 2:7

The birth of God's Son is set forth in surprising fashion. What is shocking is not how elaborate the setting for his birth was, but how ordinary and humble it was when compared to the births of earthly monarchs. Surely the Son of God would be born in a pristine setting, perhaps a mansion or a palace. Yet God's Son was born in a modest setting, much like the people he came to save. In this section, Luke continues his comparison of John the Baptist and Jesus. Jesus's superiority to John continues as well. While John's birth is described in just two verses, the events surrounding Jesus's birth are described in twenty verses. While John's circumcision and naming culminated in Zechariah's *Benedictus*, Jesus's birth is announced by an angelic choir.

The story shifts from the hill country of Judea and the birth of John the Baptist to the village of Bethlehem and the birth of Jesus Christ. This passage is one of the most memorable stories in the Bible. The birth of Jesus Christ is at the heart of the Christmas story. Paul's words could not be any more true, "For you know the grace of our Lord Jesus Christ: Though he was rich, for your sake he became poor, so that by his poverty you might become rich" (2 Cor 8:9). The difficulty is that we are so familiar with the events surrounding Jesus's birth that we no longer find the story magnificently beautiful.

Luke makes three points in these verses. First, he establishes the historical context for the birth of Jesus (vv. 1–3). Second, he provides an explanation of the political circumstances explaining why Jesus's birth took place in Bethlehem rather than Nazareth (vv. 4–5). Third, he informs his readers that Bethlehem was the city of David (vv. 6–7).[1]

The Political Setting for Jesus's Birth (2:1–3)

As for the political context of Jesus's birth, Luke mentions two names: Caesar Augustus and Quirinius.[2] Caesar Augustus is the more important of the two individuals. Augustus ("exalted one") (63 BC–AD 14) was the first Roman emperor, reigning from 27 BC until his death. Born Gaius Octavius, he was the great-nephew of Julius Caesar and became Caesar's adopted son and

---

[1] For a scholarly survey of issues surrounding Jesus's birth see Stephen E. Young, "Birth of Jesus," in *Dictionary of Jesus and the Gospels*, ed. Joel B. Green, 2nd ed. (Downers Grove: IVP Academic, 2013), 72–84.

[2] For an introduction into the historical setting of Jesus's life and ministry, see Craig L. Blomberg, *Jesus and the Gospels: An Introduction and Survey* (Nashville: B&H Academic, 2009), 4–27.

heir. Before Jesus's birth, the Roman senate conferred upon him the title Augustus. Augustus was the most powerful man in the world at the time of Jesus's birth. During his reign, the Roman empire enjoyed a period of relative peace (*Pax Romana*). The importance of this will be explained below.

The second name is Quirinius. Scholars debate whether Jesus was born in Bethlehem at the time of a census "while Quirinius was governing Syria" (v. 2). Scholars agree that Quirinius held the governorship of Syria beginning in AD 6–7 and that a census was taken at the time (Acts 5:37). However, this census is much too late to be associated with the birth of Jesus, which took place before the death of Herod the Great in 4 BC.[3] At least three major approaches to this conundrum have been proposed.[4] The first suggestion is that Luke is wrong in associating Quirinius's census with the birth of Jesus. Yet Luke has indicated that he wrote his Gospel after speaking to eyewitnesses and reading other accounts of Jesus's life (1:1–4). Considering his careful historical investigation, Luke should be given the benefit of the doubt concerning his dating of the census at the time of Jesus's birth. A second possibility is to understand Luke to be referring to a census "before" (*protos*) Quirinius was governor of Syria. A third possibility is that when the census began, Quirinius was the administrator of the census and that by the time the census was completed he was the governor of Syria. This understanding

---

[3] For additional comments on the year of Jesus's birth, see "Taking a Deeper Dive" at the end of this chapter.

[4] For a thorough analysis of competing interpretations see Darrell L. Bock, *Luke*, Baker Exegetical Commentary on the New Testament, 2 vols. (Grand Rapids: Baker Academic, 1994), 1:903–9, and Craig L. Blomberg, *The Historical Reliability of the New Testament* (Nashville: B&H Academic, 2016), 60–61.

focuses on the participle translated "governing" (*hēgemoneuō*), which is a very general term and would allow for Quirinius initially to be the administrator of the census. Either one of the last two options is preferable to the first suggestion.

A less difficult question is why Joseph would travel to Bethlehem to register for a Roman census for the purpose of taxation (v. 3). The regular Roman practice was that citizens registered for a census where they resided. Possibly, exceptions were made for local customs, and the Jewish practice may well have been for individuals to register at their ancestral home.[5] A final matter for consideration is why Mary accompanied Joseph on the journey, especially when she was near giving birth. While we cannot know for certain, it is possible that Joseph did not want to leave Mary behind to face the scorn of the village since in their minds she was giving birth to an illegitimate child. The journey from Nazareth to Bethlehem would certainly be more arduous for Joseph with a pregnant wife, but the option of leaving her behind was untenable.

On the surface, the required census was ordered by Augustus, but operating behind the scenes was God's providence in moving Jesus's parents from Nazareth to Bethlehem for his birth. While Augustus may have been the most powerful man in the world, God, who sits on heaven's throne, was directing world events. Proverbs 21:1 states the matter this way, "A king's heart is like channeled water in the LORD's hand: He directs it wherever He chooses."

---

[5] Bock, *Luke*, 1:110; David E. Garland, *Luke*, Zondervan Exegetical Commentary on the New Testament (Grand Rapids: Zondervan, 2011), 119. Mark L. Strauss, *Luke*, Zondervan Illustrated Bible Backgrounds Commentary (Grand Rapids: Zondervan, 2002), 27.

Paul made a similar point concerning the timing of Jesus's birth when he wrote, "But when the set time had fully come, God sent his Son, born of a woman, born under the law" (Gal 4:4 NIV). What did Paul mean when he wrote the "time had fully come"? Approximately 2,000 years before Jesus's birth, God called Abraham and promised him that through Abraham's family line God would bless all the nations of the earth. Why did God allow so many centuries to pass from the time he made his covenant with Abraham until the fulfillment of the promise in the birth of Jesus? At the time of Jesus's birth, many circumstances in the world favored a rapid expansion of the gospel. For example, there was the *Pax Romana* (Roman peace). The Roman military could be seen throughout the empire, keeping the empire at peace and permitting missionaries to travel safely. *Koine* ("Common") Greek was spoken throughout much of the empire, thus permitting Christian missionaries to share the gospel in a language understood by large numbers of people in varied places. In addition, as seen in the book of Acts, there were many Gentile God-fearers who worshiped on the fringes of the Jewish synagogues. These God-fearers were not Gentile proselytes (fully converted to Judaism) but were Gentiles attracted to Judaism because of its monotheism, high ethical standards, and possession of written Scriptures. These God-fearers were receptive to Paul's gospel preaching of salvation by faith apart from the works of the law. Therefore, during a period of approximately a decade (AD 48–57), Paul established churches in four Roman provinces. Paul wrote to the church at Rome, "So from Jerusalem all the way around to Illyricum, I have fully proclaimed the gospel of Christ" (Rom 15:19 NIV). Clearly, God had orchestrated world events in preparation for Jesus's birth.

Ancient Prophecy Fulfilled (2:4–5)

The main theological purpose of these verses is to show that Jesus was born in the city of David. Bethlehem ("house of bread") was at least a four-to-five-day journey from Nazareth, depending on weather conditions. The small town was located roughly five miles from Jerusalem. Approximately seven hundred years before Jesus's birth, the prophet Micah predicted the Messiah would be born in Bethlehem: "But as for you, Bethlehem Ephrathah, Too little to be among the clans of Judah, From you One will come forth for Me to be ruler in Israel. His times of coming forth are from long ago, From the days of eternity" (Mic 5:2 NASB).

Micah had a deep concern regarding the nation's future. Micah and the prophets understood the Messiah to be the nation's only hope. Micah knew the location of the Messiah's birth, but he did not know the time. The Old Testament prophets saw the shadows of the Coming One, but they did not see him with perfect clarity.

As striking as Micah's prophecy is that the Messiah would be born in Bethlehem, the thought that the child coming forth "from the days of eternity" is equally important. As John's prologue makes perfectly clear, Jesus's birth in Bethlehem was not the beginning of his existence. The Messiah would be a ruler whose life would extend from the eternal past into a glorious, endless future. Jesus made a similar statement about himself when he said, "Truly I tell you . . . before Abraham was, I am" (John 8:58).[6]

---

[6] For a fuller discussion on Mic 5:2 see chapter 12.

From Heavenly Riches to Earthly Rags (2:6–7)

The simplicity of Luke's description of Jesus's birth emphasizes its humble setting. The reference to Jesus being Mary's "first-born" is not intended to negate the fact that Mary would give birth to other children but to emphasize that Jesus possessed all the rights and responsibilities of a firstborn son. Mary wrapped Jesus in strips of cloth ("swaddling clothes," KJV) to keep his limbs straight.[7] She then laid him in a manger (*phatnē*), a feeding trough for animals. Luke states the reason for laying him in the manger was because "there was no guest room (*katalyma*) available to them" ("no room for them in the inn," KJV). The picture in the minds of many is that Joseph and Mary were turned away from something akin to a modern motel or "inn." The image of a heartless hotel owner is not found in the biblical text.

The reality is more like a private residence or a public shelter where travelers would spend the night.[8] Later in Luke's Gospel, he uses a different word for a public inn (*pandocheion*) when he recounts the parable of the good Samaritan (Luke 10:34). The term *katalyma* ("guest room," CSB) is used in Luke when referring to the "upper room" or "guest room" where Jesus will celebrate the Passover with his disciples (Luke 22:11; cf. Mark 14:14). Bethlehem would have been overrun with visitors who had traveled to register at their ancestral home.

The traditional site of Jesus's birth is the present-day Church of the Nativity in Manger Square in Bethlehem. The church was constructed in the fourth century over a cave. The thought that

---

[7] Robert H. Stein, *Luke*, vol. 24, The New American Commentary (Nashville: B&H Academic, 1992), 107.

[8] Strauss, *Luke*, 25.

Jesus was born in a cave where animals were kept is quite early.[9] When one looks past the cathedral and focuses on the simple setting in the cathedral's basement, the humble nature of Jesus's birth comes into focus. Kenneth Bailey, however, argues that Luke's language is better understood to describe Jesus's birth taking place in the lower level of a home.[10] Ancient homes in Palestine often had two levels. The lower level was reserved for any animals that would be kept inside due to weather or protection from predators. The family slept on the second level. Considering that Joseph may have had distant relatives in Bethlehem, the possibility exists that while there was no room for Mary and Joseph on the upper level of the home, they stayed on the lower level surrounded by several animals. Whether the family lodged in the lower level of a home, where animals resided at night, a cave where animals slept, or something more similar to an enclosed pen that served the same purpose, the location was not one where you would typically find a child being born, especially Israel's Messiah. Everything about the birthplace of Jesus reflects the lowly status of one who "did not come to be served, but to serve" (Mark 10:45). Whether Jesus was born in a home, cave, or stable, the first Christmas story looks considerably different from many contemporary depictions of it.

The following is Ken Gire's attempt to describe the scene, not as depicted in a Renaissance painting or a church Christmas pageant but how the scene might have looked to the eyes of a first-century bystander.

---

[9] *Protoevangelium of James* 18; Justin Martyr, *Dialogue with Trypho* 78.4.

[10] Kenneth E. Bailey, *Jesus through Middle Eastern Eyes* (Downers Grove: IVP Academic, 2008), 25–37.

By the time they arrive, the small hamlet of Bethlehem is swollen from an influx of travelers. The inn is packed, people feeling lucky if they were able to negotiate even a small space on the floor. Now it is late, everyone is asleep, and there is no room. But fortunately, the innkeeper is not all shekels and mites. True, his stable is crowded with his guests' animals, but if they could squeeze out a little privacy there, they were welcome to it. Joseph looks over at Mary, whose attention is concentrated on fighting a contraction. "We'll take it," he tells the innkeeper without hesitation. The night is still when Joseph creeks open the stable door. As he does, a chorus of barn animals makes discordant note of the intrusion. The stench is pungent and humid, as there have not been enough hours in the day to tend the guests, let alone the livestock. A small oil lamp, lent them by the innkeeper, flickers to dance shadows on the walls. A disquieting place for a woman in the throes of childbirth. Far from home. Far from family. Far from what she had expected for her firstborn. But Mary makes no complaint. It is relief just to finally get off the donkey. She leans back against the wall, her feet swollen, back aching, contractions growing stronger and closer together. Joseph's eyes dart around the stable. Not a minute to lose. Quickly. A feeding trough would have to make do for a crib. Hay would serve as a mattress. Blankets? Blankets? Ah, his robe. That would do. And those rags hung out to dry would help. A gripping contraction doubles Mary over and sends him racing for a bucket of water . . . A scream from Mary knifes through the calm of the silent night. Joseph returns, breathless, water sloshing from the wooden bucket . . . Sweat pours from Mary's contorted face as Joseph, the most unlikely midwife in all Judea, rushes to her side. The involuntary contractions are not enough, and Mary has to push with all her strength . . . Joseph places a garment beneath her, and with a final push and a long sigh her labor is over. The Messiah has arrived.[11]

Is this how the birth of Jesus happened? We do not know for certain. But Gire's depiction is certainly closer to reality than paintings where Mary and Jesus have halos over their heads!

Final Reflections

At least two truths stand out from this passage for further consideration. First, God's ways and timing are often different from our own. God waited approximately one thousand years between his covenant with Abraham and his covenant with David. At various points during those centuries, it appeared God's plans would never come to pass. Yet God was orchestrating events so that a man after God's own heart would become the unlikely king of Israel. At many points in the next thousand years, God's people must have wondered what God was doing. Again, God was orchestrating world circumstances for the birth of Jesus and the worldwide spread of the gospel. In the fullness of time, when Caesar Augustus ruled much of the ancient world, God's Son was conceived in a virgin's womb in the village of Nazareth. God ordained a Roman emperor to declare a census be taken that required Joseph (and Mary) to travel from Nazareth to

---

[11] Ken Gire, *Moments with the Savior: Learning to Love* (Grand Rapids: Zondervan, 1989), 3–4.

Bethlehem, where Jesus would be born. Jesus's Bethlehem birth fulfilled a prophecy made five hundred years earlier. This recounting of God's sovereignty in action should bring us comfort and not fear. As we contemplate the future, God's people can rest assured that God, not rogue regimes and evil empires, will be the ultimate determiner of world events.

Second, as with every passage in the Birth and Infancy narratives, Jesus is the most important person. As we reflect on this scene, we go back to Paul's words quoted at the beginning of this chapter, "For you know the grace of our Lord Jesus Christ: Though he was rich, for your sake he became poor, so that by his poverty you might become rich" (2 Cor 8:9). Why would one so great and glorious allow himself to be born in obscurity in such a lowly setting? The creator of the world, worshipped by the angels of heaven, found himself as a helpless baby, surrounded by the noise of animals in a stable. The only answer as to why Jesus would submit to these circumstances is his love for his Father and his love for those he came to save. The incarnation of Jesus the Messiah is a reminder that you are valuable to God, more valuable than you could ever imagine. On that first Christmas night, heaven's king was held by a woman he created, who nursed him, changed him, and lovingly embraced him. Jesus would one day say, "Foxes have dens, and birds of the sky have nests, but the Son of Man has no place to lay his head" (Matt 8:20). The homelessness of Jesus, in a very real sense, was true from the beginning of his earthly life.

A Christmas Hymn of Response

Silent night, holy night,
All is calm, all is bright
Round yon Virgin Mother and Child!

Holy infant so tender and mild,
Sleep in heavenly peace,
Sleep in heavenly peace.

Silent night, holy night
All is calm, all is bright
Round yon Virgin Mother and Child
Holy infant so tender and mild
Sleep in heavenly peace
Sleep in heavenly peace.[12]

Taking a Deeper Dive: The Year of Jesus's Birth

When one learns that Jesus's birth is dated sometime between 6 and 4 BC, it seems odd. How could Jesus be born BC ("before Christ")? The division of the calendar into BC and AD (*anno domini* = "in the year of our Lord") dates to the Gregorian calendar in the 1500s.[13] The Gregorian calendar was based upon the work of the sixth-century monk, Dionysius Exiguus, who miscalculated the date of Jesus's birth by at least four years.[14] Both Matthew and Luke date Jesus's birth during the reign of Herod the Great (Matt 2:1; Luke 1:5). Herod died in 4 BC. The fact

---

[12] Franz Xaver Gruber, "Silent Night, Holy Night," 1816, *Baptist Hymnal*, #91.

[13] See Blomberg, *Jesus and the Gospels*, 222. For a more comprehensive discussion of the dating of the birth of Jesus, see Jeannine K. Brown and Harold W. Hoehner, "Chronology," in *Dictionary of Jesus and the Gospels*, ed. Joel B. Green, 2nd ed. (Downers Grove: IVP Academic, 2013), 134–38.

[14] Mark L. Strauss, *Four Portraits, One Jesus: A Survey of Jesus and the Gospels* (Grand Rapids: Zondervan, 2011), 405.

that Herod ordered the murder of all baby boys two years of age and younger in the vicinity of Bethlehem suggests a date for Jesus's birth between 7 and 6 BC, but little evidence exists beyond this to be more precise.

The traditional date of the day of Jesus's birth in the Western church is December 25. The date held by the Eastern churches is January 6. The traditional date may go back as far as Constantine.[15] Some may point to the fact that the shepherds were in the fields to dismiss a possible winter date for Christ's birth, but, truthfully, we simply do not know the exact date of Jesus's birth.

---

[15] Strauss, *Four Portraits*, 406.

CHAPTER 9

THE SONG OF THE ANGELS

LUKE 2:8–20

> "Today in the city of David a Savior was born for
> you, who is the Messiah, the Lord."
> —Luke 2:11

At this point in the unfolding of events, there was another unexpected turn of events. Instead of Jesus's birth being announced to individuals of governmental power or religious significance, the announcement was made to lowly shepherds. Once again, we learn that God's ways are not our ways. Paul wrote this to the Corinthians:

Brothers and sisters, consider your calling: Not many were wise from a human perspective, not many powerful, not many of noble birth. Instead, God has chosen what is foolish in the world to shame the wise, and God has chosen what is weak in the world to shame the strong. God has chosen what is insignificant and despised in the world—what is viewed as nothing—to bring to nothing what is viewed as something. (1 Cor 1:26–28)

An Unlikely Setting (2:8)

The announcement of the birth of royal children is typically made to the elites of society, but Jesus's birth was announced to outcasts.[1] Everything that took place on that first Christmas is the opposite of what would be written in a textbook on human greatness.

The shepherds were out in fields protecting their sheep from thieves and predators.[2] Often shepherds lived outdoors with their flock in the warmer months, but some rabbinic evidence indicates year-round grazing.[3] In later Jewish writings, shepherds were said to be thieves and liars.[4] However, in the Old Testament, God calls himself the Shepherd of his people (Pss 95:7; 79:13; 100:3). In John 10, Jesus described himself as the Good Shepherd (10:11, 14). Furthermore, some of the most significant figures in the Old Testament were shepherds at one time—Moses, Abraham, and David. While shepherds in Jesus's day were not as notorious as many have thought, they did live somewhat on the fringes of Jewish society. Shepherds could spend long periods of time away from home caring for their flock. This meant they may not have been able to attend synagogue services as regularly as others. Furthermore, they had to handle the carcasses of dead animals, which rendered them

---

[1] Robert H. Stein, *Luke*, vol. 24, The New American Commentary (Nashville: B&H Academic, 1992), 108.

[2] The traditional location is known as "Shepherds Field," located about two miles outside Bethlehem. See Raymond E. Brown, *The Birth of the Messiah: A Commentary on the Infancy Narratives in Matthew and Luke* (Garden City, NY: Doubleday, 1977), 401.

[3] Mark L. Strauss, *Luke*, Zondervan Illustrated Bible Backgrounds Commentary (Grand Rapids: Zondervan, 2002), 27.

[4] Strauss, *Luke*, 26.

ritually unclean. The angel's announcement to the shepherds foreshadowed the fact that Jesus would love those people many tend to ignore. In Jesus's Nazareth sermon he quoted Isa 61:1–2 as a programmatic statement of his ministry.

"The Spirit of the Lord is upon Me,
Because He anointed Me to bring good news to the poor.
He has sent Me to proclaim release to captives,
And recovery of sight to the blind,
To set free those who are oppressed,
To proclaim the favorable year of the Lord." (Luke 4:18–19 NASB)

The theme of Jesus's ministry to outcasts is important throughout Luke's Gospel. Jesus called a tax collector to be a disciple, forgave an immoral woman of her sins, declared a chief tax collector to be a genuine "son of Abraham," and forgave a dying criminal hanging on the cross beside him (Luke 5:27–28; 7:37–50; 19:1–10; 23:40–43). When asked why he ate with tax collectors and sinners, Jesus replied, "It is not those who are healthy who need a doctor, but those who are sick. I have not come to call the righteous, but sinners to repentance" (Luke 5:31–32).

Perhaps there were few who felt more like outcasts than Luke and his Gentile readers. Throughout his Gospel, Luke takes every opportunity to communicate to his Gentile readers that Jesus came to be the Savior of all people—both Jew and Gentile. Jesus's concern for all people is demonstrated by the fact that he ministered to people from different classes, races, and genders. A few examples will demonstrate Jesus's desire to be the Savior of the world. Jesus's genealogy in Luke's Gospel goes back to Adam, a Gentile. This is unlike Matthew's genealogy of Jesus, which begins with Abraham, the father of the Jewish people, and culminates with

Jesus, the Messiah of the Jewish people. Luke's point in tracing Jesus's lineage back to Adam is to show that Jesus is related to all people and not just the Jewish people. Jesus compared his ministry to Elijah and Elisha (4:23–27). Elijah ministered to the widow of Zarephath and her son, while Elisha ministered to Naaman the Syrian. These comparisons caused those who heard them to run Jesus out of town. Jesus healed a Roman centurion's servant (7:1–10). Jesus told a parable with a hated Samaritan being the hero of the story (10:30–37). Jesus healed a Samaritan leper (17:12–19). These examples are sufficient to show that the coming of Jesus was to bring salvation to the world—both Jews and Gentiles.

A Shocking Announcement (2:9–14)

At first, just a single angel appeared to the shepherds. The angel was not named because the message matters more than the messenger. The angel's message was heaven's announcement of the significance of Jesus's birth. The announcement was preceded by the manifestation of "the glory of the Lord," which would have illuminated the night sky. We can hardly imagine the fear that must have gripped the shepherds' hearts. "The glory of the Lord" refers to the manifestation of God's powerful and majestic presence. The word "glory" (*doxa*) is used in the Septuagint when God's presence settled on Mount Sinai, the tabernacle, and the Temple (Exod 24:16–17; 40:34–35; 1 Kgs 8:11).

Angels continued to play an important role in the Birth and Infancy narratives.[5] Once again, we need to remind ourselves

---

[5] For a more comprehensive discussion on the topic of angels, see Crispin Fletcher-Louis, "Angels," in *Dictionary of Jesus and the Gospels*, ed. Joel B. Green, 2nd ed. (Downers Grove: IVP Academic, 2013), 11–17.

that angels do not look like the Precious Moments figurines on our grandmother's shelves. Nor are angels anything like the bumbling character Clarence in the heartwarming Christmas movie, *A Wonderful Life*. Among some Christians, there is much confusion over what angels are and what they do. For example, some think that people become angels when they die, but they most certainly do not. In the Bible, angels are not the major characters, but they do play an important role in certain moments in redemptive history. Therefore, what are angels, and what do they do? First, God created angels as spiritual beings; that is, they do not have physical bodies like human beings, although sometimes they appear in the Bible taking human form (Mark 16:5). Second, some of the angels created by God joined in Satan's rebellion against God and are called demons or evil spirits (Mark 1:23). The final destiny of Satan and demons is eternal hell (Rev 20:10).[6] Third, God created angels to be his servants. Angels worship God and carry out his bidding (Rev 4–5; 8:6). Angels are his messengers of hope, good news, and judgment (Matt 28:1–7; Gen 19:1–17). Fourth, the Bible teaches that angels are present when Christian congregations gather for worship (1 Cor 11:10). Fifth, the author of Hebrews said some believers have been unaware when entertaining angels (Heb 13:2). While angels are not the most important characters in the storyline of Scripture, they do play a crucial role in the Bible.

The significance of Jesus's birth was heard in the angel's words, "Good news of great joy for all the people." Each aspect

---

[6] For a more complete discussion of Satan and demons in the Bible see William F. Cook and Chuck Lawless, *Spiritual Warfare in the Storyline of Scripture: A Biblical, Theological, and Practical Approach* (Nashville: B&H Academic, 2019).

of the message merits consideration. First, the words "proclaim good news" (*euangelizomai*) became a way of referring to the gospel proclamation (the following is a sampling of the use of the phrase in Luke and Acts: Luke 1:19; 2:10; 3:18; 4:18, 43; 7:22; 8:1; 9:6; 16:16; 20:1; Acts 5:42; 8:12; 10:36; 14:15). Stein makes the interesting point that this verb is found eleven times in the Gospels and that ten of these are found in Luke.[7] Centuries earlier, Isaiah made similar declarations.

How beautiful on the mountains are the feet of the herald, who proclaims peace, who brings news of good things, who proclaims salvation, who says to Zion, "Your God reigns!" (Isa 52:7)

The Spirit of the Lord GOD is upon me, because the LORD has anointed me to bring good news to the poor. He has sent me to heal the brokenhearted, to proclaim liberty to captives and freedom to prisoners. (Isa 61:1)

Next, the good news brings great joy. Joy is a missing jewel in the lives of many believers. Joy is a fruit of the Spirit (Gal 5:22). The word joy is used more in Luke's Gospel than in Matthew's and Mark's Gospels combined. The message is of "good news of great joy."[8] Along with the thought of joy, praise is a related theme in Luke's Gospel. Luke's Birth narrative is punctuated by expressions of joy and song.

As we have seen, Luke's first two chapters record some wonderful songs of praise: Mary's *Magnificat* (1:46–55), Zechariah's

---

[7] Stein, *Luke*, 108.

[8] For more on the theme of joy, see "Taking a Deeper Dive" at the end of this chapter.

Benedictus (1:68–79), the angels' *Gloria* (2:14), and Simeon's *Nunc Dimittis* (2:29–32). The message of joy and rejoicing begins early in Luke's narrative with Gabriel's message to Zechariah concerning the birth of John: "There will be joy and delight for you, and many will rejoice at his birth" (1:14). When Elizabeth encountered Mary, the baby in Elizabeth's womb "leaped for joy" (1:43–44). Mary's song begins with the words, "My soul magnifies the Lord, and my spirit rejoices in God my Savior" (1:46–47). When Zechariah's voice returned after approximately nine months of muteness, his first words were praise to God (1:64). Later in Luke's Gospel, Simeon blessed God when he took the baby Jesus into his arms (2:28). In such ways, Luke makes it abundantly clear that the coming of Jesus was a cause for great rejoicing and praise.

The joy and praise permeating the Birth and Infancy narrative are true throughout the remainder of Luke's Gospel. Jesus "rejoiced greatly in the Holy Spirit" (10:21 NASB). Rejoicing abounds when those who are lost are found (15:6, 9, 32). The theme of joy culminates the book at Jesus's ascension. The disciples "returned to Jerusalem with great joy" (24:52). Much more could be said on the topic of joy and praise in Luke's Gospel, but these references are sufficient to demonstrate the joy Jesus brings into a person's life. The question is, "What do we know of the joy of the Lord in our daily lives?"

We now return to the angel's message to the shepherds. The angel's message is "for all people." The word translated "people" (*laos*) here refers specifically to the Jewish people when used in Luke's Gospel.[9] Jesus's coming was good news for the Jewish

---

[9] David E. Garland, *Luke*, Zondervan Exegetical Commentary on the New Testament (Grand Rapids: Zondervan, 2011), 122.

people, regardless of their gender, education, or social standing. As Stein points out, the good news was ultimately for Gentiles as well as Jews, as Luke makes clear in Acts.[10] But here Luke was thinking primarily of the Jewish people. The angel's word "today" suggests the long wait for the Messiah had ended. The kingdom of God was about to be inaugurated. No longer was there any delay. The ancient whispers of a coming Savior had come to fruition—"Today."[11]

- Today . . . a Savior was born. (2:11)
- Today . . . this Scripture has been fulfilled. (4:21)
- Today . . . they were filled with awe and had seen incredible things. (5:26)
- Today . . . "it is necessary for me [Jesus] to stay at your [Zacchaeus] house." (19:5)
- Today salvation has come to this house. (19:9, 10)
- Today "you will be with me in paradise." (23:43)

Today could be the day of salvation for you or someone you love. Today could be the day you draw a line in the sand and say "No" to a particular sin—enough is enough. Today could be the day you determine you will be an instrument of healing in your fractured marriage rather than continue to contribute to the heartache and pain in your home. God's grace is available *today*, right now, for those who desire it!

The titles the angel ascribes to Jesus further highlight his identity: "Savior" (deliverer), "Christ" (Messiah), and "Lord." This is the only place in Scripture where the specific title of "Christ

---

[10] Stein, *Luke*, 108.

[11] For a fuller discussion on the thought of "Today" in Luke, see Garland, *Luke*, 123.

the Lord" is applied to Jesus, but the thought that Christ is the Lord is found elsewhere (for example, see Acts 2:36; 2 Cor 4:5). Each title carries great weight. At the time of Jesus's birth, many longed for a Messiah to deliver them from Roman domination, but Jesus came to deliver his people from bondage to Satan, sin, and death. Many looked for a Messianic Warrior, but Jesus came to be the Prince of Peace.

Twice in the New Testament Jesus is referred to as the "Savior of the world." The first reference is attributed to a group of Samaritans who met Jesus through the testimony of the infamous Samaritan woman (John 4:42). The second reference to Jesus as the Savior of the world is in 1 John 4:14: "And we have seen and we testify that the Father has sent his Son as the world's Savior." However, many places in the New Testament state the same truth in slightly different words. For example, Peter wrote, "But grow in the grace and knowledge of our Lord and Savior Jesus Christ. To him be the glory both now and to the day of eternity" (2 Pet 3:18).[12]

The angel associated Jesus's birth with the city of David; however, he did not mention Bethlehem by name. When people of the day heard "the city of David," they thought of Jerusalem. As we have seen from our discussion of Mic 5:2, the Messiah was to be born in Bethlehem, not Jerusalem. Bethlehem was more of a rural village than the likely location for the birth of a king. Bethlehem, rather than Jerusalem, is another example of the topsy-turvy nature of these monumental events.

When the angel spoke of Jesus as "Lord," he meant much more by his use of the term than the shepherds could have

---

[12] For additional thoughts on "Jesus as Savior," see Final Reflections at the end of this chapter.

possibly understood. The shepherds would have thought that the child was their master in the sense that he was their Messiah. The angel, however, knew better than the shepherds. The angel used the title "Lord" in reference to Jesus's deity. The child lying in a manger created the angels. In addition, Luke's readers would have had a deeper understanding than the shepherds had initially.

Once again, a sign was provided to the recipients of an angelic message. Zechariah's sign was his muteness, Mary's sign was Elizabeth's pregnancy, and the shepherds' sign was a baby wrapped in cloths and lying in a manger—such an unlikely place for the birth of a child, especially God's Son. While other babies may have been born in Bethlehem that night, there would be only one lying in a manger, and the shepherds would have no problem eventually finding him.

As unexpected as the appearance of the first angel, suddenly a multitude of angels appeared in the dark sky praising God. The angelic choir's brief song is called the *Gloria in Excelsis Deo* ("Glory to God in the highest"), from the first words of the Latin Vulgate translation. They promise God's peace to those on whom God's favor rests ("with whom God is pleased," NLT).[13] The Messiah-King came on his first visit to make peace possible between sinners and a holy God. The prophet Isaiah makes a similar point.

> For a child will be born for us,
> a son will be given to us,
> and the government will be on his shoulders.

---

[13] The CSB translation "peace on earth to people he favors" is to be preferred to the KJV's more familiar translation of "good will toward men." The KJV translation is based on inferior manuscripts. The phrase refers to God's favor bestowed on his people.

He will be named
Wonderful Counselor, Mighty God,
Eternal Father, Prince of Peace.
The dominion will be vast,
and its prosperity will never end.
He will reign on the throne of David
and over his kingdom,
to establish and sustain it
with justice and righteousness from now on and forever.
The zeal of the Lord of Armies will accomplish this.
    (Isa 9:6–7)

Just when many Jewish people were waiting for a Messiah that would initiate a war against Rome, God sends "the Prince of Peace." The price for peace with God was greater than anyone could imagine. The prophet Isaiah wrote,

But he was pierced for our transgressions,
he was crushed for our iniquities;
the punishment that brought us peace was on him,
and by his wounds we are healed. (Isa 53:5 NIV)

Despite the calmness of the night, a war was being initiated; the kingdom of God was invading the kingdom of darkness. The One who came to bring life is the very One who would give his life for the redemption of sinners.

A Proper Response to Christ's Birth (2:15–20)

The final verses of this section highlight several important truths. First, while the angelic response to the birth of Jesus was to *sing*, the shepherd's response was to *seek* for the child (v. 15). Later we will see that neither Herod nor the religious leadership made the short trip from Jerusalem to Bethlehem to see if what the wise men were saying was true. The shepherds wasted no time in following the angel's directive, setting out immediately to find the newborn child. The shepherds understood God was speaking to them through the angelic message.

Second, the shepherds found everything just as they had been told—the baby lying in a manger. God was superintending these events, and everything was taking place as God had planned. No one could have anticipated God ordaining events as he did, such as his Son's humble birthplace or the first announcement being made to *nameless* shepherds. From the very beginning of the incarnation, Jesus demonstrated for his followers that the first will be last and the last will be first.

Third, the shepherds did not keep their discovery a secret but shared the good news with anyone who would listen. Surely, Luke intended the same for his readers—to share with anyone who would listen the story of Jesus the King and the salvation he brings.

Fourth, the reference to Mary treasuring these things in her heart may be a subtle indication that Luke learned about these events from Mary or someone very close to her. Even though Mary and Joseph had been given much information on the events they were experiencing, the arrival of the shepherds would have shocked them. The shepherds' description of the angelic host was totally unexpected to them. Mary and Joseph were alone in a town they likely had never visited. Mary gave birth in a stable surrounded by animals, with no family or friends present. They must have been stunned by the arrival of the shepherds and the recounting of the message of the angelic host. If they had felt alone while Jesus was being born, they must have been greatly encouraged in the hours following the birth. God's graciousness was on full display in the dingy stable.

Finally, the shepherds returned to their flock "glorifying and praising God." As we have seen, the thought of praising God is a crucial theme in Luke's Gospel. The love of singing at Christmas goes back to the first Christmas with the singing of the angels and the praising of God by the shepherds. Nothing can enliven a Christmas filled with the hustle and bustle of the season more than singing the songs of Christmas.

Final Reflections

The thought that the child born in a Bethlehem stable is the Savior of the world is as glorious as it is surprising. The word *Savior* means someone who saves or delivers another from danger. Jesus's name means "Yahweh saves." In the Old Testament, God is frequently referred to as the Savior of his people. Psalm 18:46 reads, "The LORD lives! Praise be to my Rock! Exalted be God my Savior!" (NIV). Psalm 38:22 speaks similarly of God: "Come quickly to help me, my Lord and my Savior" (NIV).

What does Jesus rescue us from, and what does Jesus rescue us for? If we are to grasp fully Jesus's role as Savior, we must understand our own spiritual condition apart from him. The Bible teaches that all people have sinned against God (Rom 3:23). "There is no one righteous, not even one" (Rom 3:9–10). Paul states the matter of our spiritual condition clearly in Eph 2:1–5, where he says that outside of Christ people are spiritually dead, enslaved, and condemned, but God has graciously provided a means by which we can be reconciled to him through his Son. Apart from Jesus, we can never be in a right relationship with God.

Our spiritual condition apart from Christ is why Jesus's incarnation is so important. Being God, Jesus is perfectly holy, and in his humanity he lived a perfectly righteous life; therefore, he did not deserve to die (2 Cor 5:21). Jesus chose to die on the cross for us, paying the penalty for our sin (Rom 6:23; 1 Pet 2:24; 1 John 2:2). Three days later he rose from the dead, confirming his victory over Satan, sin, and death. By putting your faith in Christ, you can be reconciled to God. If you don't know Jesus as your Savior and Lord, you need to be rescued. Jesus came to save you.

Jesus not only saved us *from* God's righteous judgment, but he saved us *for* something. Jesus saves us so that we can be adopted into God's family and become part of his church (John 3:16–18; Rom 5:10). Jesus saves us so that we can be a part of a worldwide missionary movement (Matt 28:16–20). As you can see, Jesus saves us for so much more than just taking us to heaven, as important as that is. Jesus saves us to be salt and light to a world in darkness and decay (Matt 5:13–16). Jesus is indeed the Savior of the world. But is he your Savior?

A Christmas Hymn of Response

Hark! the herald angels sing
"Glory to the new-born king;
Peace on earth, and mercy mild;
God and sinners reconciled."
Joyful, all ye nations rise,
Join the triumph of the skies;
With angelic hosts proclaim,
"Christ is born in Bethlehem!"
Hark! The herald angels sing,

"Glory to the new-born king."

Hail the heav'n-born Prince of Peace!
Hail the Sun of righteousness!
Light and life to all He brings,
Ris'n with healing in His wings.
Mild He lays His glory by,
Born that man no more may die,
Born to raise the sons of earth,
Born to give them second birth.
Hark! The herald angels sing,
"Glory to the new-born king."

Hark! The herald angels sing
"Glory to the new-born king
Peace on earth and mercy mild
God and sinners reconciled"
Joyful all ye nations rise
Join the triumph of the skies
With angelic host proclaim
"Christ is born in Bethlehem"
Hark! The herald angels sing
"Glory to the new-born king"
"Glory to the new-born king."[14]

Taking a Deeper Dive: The Joy of Christmas

For many people Christmas is one of the loneliest times of the
year. A season filled with family gatherings is very difficult for

[14] Charles Wesley, "Hark the Herald Angels Sing," 1739, *Baptist Hymnal*, # 88.

those without family. For others, the joy of Christmas seems to dissipate as quickly as the holiday ends. Joy (*chara*) (1:14; 2:10; 8:13; 10:17; 15:7, 10; 24:41, 52; Acts 8:8; 12:14; 13:52; 15:3) and rejoicing (*agalliaō*) (1:47; 10:21; Acts 2:26; 16:34), as is the verb *chairō* (rejoice) (1:14; 6:23; 10:20; 13:17; 15:5, 32; 19:6, 37; Acts 5:41; 8:39; 11:23; 13:48; 15:31), are important words in Luke's Gospel and especially in his Birth and Infancy narrative.[15] Luke wanted his readers to understand that some of the joy of the world to come has invaded this world with the coming of Jesus. As evident in the above references, the thought of joy runs through both of Luke's volumes. Joy is an often-overlooked blessing of Christ's coming.

As we have seen, Luke's Birth and Infancy narratives are filled with singing—Mary's *Magnificat* (1:46–55), Zechariah's *Benedictus* (1:68–79), the angel's *Gloria* (2:14), and Simeon's *Nunc Dimittis* (2:29–32). Each of these four songs radiates with the joy of Jesus. If we turn our attention momentarily to Acts, we discover singing in a most unusual place—a jail cell (Acts 16:25). After Paul and Silas were arrested and beaten, they were thrown into the inner prison, and their feet were fastened in the stocks. Rather than focusing on their circumstances, they sang to the Lord, and the Holy Spirit used their singing in the life of the Philippian jailer, who gave his heart to Christ. The last place one would have expected to hear singing and rejoicing would have been in a Roman jail. The last place one would anticipate a person coming to Jesus would be a jailer in a Roman jail.

Luke does not waste any time introducing the concept of joy in his Gospel. In 1:14, Gabriel told Zechariah that he and

---

[15] For a book-length treatment, see William Morrice, *Joy in the New Testament* (Grand Rapids: Eerdmans, 1985).

Elizabeth would have joy (*chara*) and gladness (*agalliaō*) at the birth of John and that many would rejoice (*chairō*) at his coming. When Elizabeth encountered Mary, Elizabeth told her that the baby leaped in her (Elizabeth's) womb for joy (1:43–44). Mary's *Magnificat* begins, "And my spirit has rejoiced in God my Savior" (1:47 NASB). Luke makes abundantly clear that the arrival of Jesus fills people with joy.

If we dig deeper into this idea in Luke's Birth and Infancy narrative, we discover this crucial theme throughout. For example, when one sinner repents, there is great joy in heaven (15:7, 10). When the prodigal son returns home, the father threw a great banquet. When his older son refused to attend, the father said to the older brother, "But we had to celebrate and rejoice, because this brother of yours was dead and is alive again; he was lost and is found" (15:32). After a successful short-term mission trip, the seventy-two returned in joy (10:17), and Jesus "rejoiced in the Holy Spirit" (10:21). In the final scene of Luke's Gospel, the disciples are described as worshiping Jesus at his ascension and as they returned to Jerusalem "with great joy. And they were continually in the temple praising God" (24:52–53). Beginning with the Birth and Infancy narrative and concluding with the ascension, Luke's Gospel is a Gospel of joy.

What's true in Luke is equally true in Acts. Luke's second volume carries on the theme of joy as a characteristic mark of the church. The church of Jesus Christ is a rejoicing people. The disciples rejoice that they are considered worthy to suffer for Jesus's name (Acts 5:41). There is great joy when the gospel comes to Samaria (8:8). The Ethiopian eunuch goes "on his way rejoicing" after trusting in Christ and being baptized by Philip (8:39). When Barnabas sees all the good things the Lord has done in Antioch, he rejoices (11:23). The disciples are "filled with joy and with the Holy Spirit" (13:52 NIV). The conversion of Gentiles brings "great joy to all the brothers and sisters" (15:3). The point of this long excursion is that the church of Jesus Christ should be a joy-filled people. For Luke, joy begins with the arrival of Jesus.

CHAPTER 10

THE JOY OF SIMEON AND ANNA

LUKE 2:21–40

> "Now, Master,
> you can dismiss your servant in peace,
> as you promised.
> For my eyes have seen your salvation.
> You have prepared it
> in the presence of all peoples—
> a light for revelation to the Gentiles
> and glory to your people Israel."
> —Luke 2:29–32

The setting now shifts from Bethlehem to Jerusalem. Jerusalem plays an important role in Luke's Gospel. The Gentile, Luke, refers to Jerusalem thirty-one times in the Gospel and another fifty-nine times in Acts. This usage compares to eleven times in Mark and fifteen times in Matthew. Luke brackets his Gospel with stories taking place at the temple in Jerusalem. The opening story describes Zechariah serving God in the Jerusalem Temple

(1:8–23), and the final story describes the disciples returning to Jerusalem and going to the temple after Jesus's ascension
(24:52–53). Luke is the only Gospel that describes Jesus being
taken to Jerusalem as an infant and then again at the age of twelve
(2:21–23; 41–50). While Matthew includes Jesus's temptation at
the temple as the second of his three temptations, Luke places
the temple temptation last (Matt 4:5–7; Luke 4:9–13). Luke has
likely rearranged the order of the second and third temptation
to make a theological point. At times, the Gospel writers will
arrange their material thematically rather than chronologically.
If this understanding is correct, then Luke placed the Jerusalem
temple temptation last to highlight it. For the devil to tempt the
holy Son of God in Israel's holiest city and at her holiest of sights
demonstrates the devil's diabolical nature. The central section
of Luke's Gospel focuses on Jesus's journey to Jerusalem. Luke
repeats several times that Jesus is moving toward Jerusalem (9:51;
13:22; 17:11; 19:11, 27). Yet, sadly, when Jesus arrived at Jerusalem,
the people rejected their king. As Jesus sat on a donkey on Palm
Sunday, looking out over Jerusalem from the Mount of Olives, he
broke down and wept. The city of Jerusalem would be overthrown
and demolished by the Romans in AD 70 (19:41–44), all because
they missed the time of their visitation by God's Son (19:41–42).
John's words could not have been more true, "He came to his own,
and his own people did not receive him" (John 1:11).

This portion of Luke's narrative can be divided into four
sections. First, Joseph and Mary proved themselves to be committed to obeying God's word (vv. 21–24). As mentioned above,
they took Jesus to Jerusalem in fulfillment of several ancient ceremonies. Second, a man by the name of Simeon stepped out of
history's shadow and onto the world stage for a moment (vv. 25–
35). His prophetic words highlight the significance of the young

child. Third, an elderly widow spoke wonderful words of prophecy to anyone who would listen concerning the baby Jesus (vv. 36–38). Fourth, after faithfully fulfilling all the requirements of God's law, the family returned to Nazareth (vv. 39–40). Unlike Matthew, Luke does not describe the family settling down in Bethlehem or making the hasty journey to Egypt.

Ancient Ceremonies (2:21–24)

We see in this opening section why God chose Joseph and Mary to be Jesus's earthly parents. The couple demonstrate great obedience to God's Word.[1] Everything God's Word required a young family to do, Mary and Joseph did.[2] The following verses demonstrate their faithfulness.

- Mary and Joseph had Jesus circumcised on the eighth day as required by the law of God. (v. 21)
- Mary and Joseph named their son Jesus, as directed by the angel. (v. 21)
- Mary observed her required days of purification. (v. 22)
- Mary and Joseph took Jesus to Jerusalem to present him to the Lord as their firstborn son. (vv. 22–23)
- Before they left Bethlehem, Mary and Joseph "completed everything according to the law of the Lord." (v. 39)

The circumcision of Jesus was the first of three ancient ceremonies the family participated in. Circumcision took

---

[1] David E. Garland, *Luke*, Zondervan Exegetical Commentary on the New Testament (Grand Rapids: Zondervan, 2011), 138–39.

[2] Darrell L. Bock, *Luke*, Baker Exegetical Commentary on the New Testament, 2 vols. (Grand Rapids: Baker Academic, 1994), 1:234–35.

place on the eighth day after the birth of a son. The origin
of circumcision in the Jewish faith goes back to Abraham.
Approximately two thousand years before Jesus's birth, God
instructed Abraham to circumcise males on the eighth day.
Genesis 17:10–12 reads,

> "This is my covenant between me and you and your off-
> spring after you, which you are to keep: Every one of
> your males must be circumcised. You must circumcise
> the flesh of your foreskin to serve as a sign of the cove-
> nant between me and you. Throughout your generations,
> every male among you is to be circumcised at eight days
> old—every male born in your household or purchased
> from any foreigner and not your offspring."

Approximately five hundred years after Abraham, God repeated
his instructions on circumcision to Moses. Leviticus 12:3 reads,
"The flesh of his foreskin must be circumcised on the eighth day."
So sacred was the ceremony of circumcision, it would be carried
out even if the eighth day fell on a Sabbath, when essentially
every unnecessary activity was forbidden. As mentioned above,
circumcision commemorated God's covenant with his people. At
the time of the circumcision, Mary and Joseph formally named
their son Jesus, the name given by the angel.

The second act of obedience to God's law is called the
"Redemption of the Firstborn." Every firstborn son was to be
presented to God one month after birth. Two relevant texts are
Exod 13:2 and Num 18:15–16:

> "Consecrate every firstborn male to me, the firstborn
> from every womb among the Israelites, both man and
> domestic animal; it is mine." (Exod 13:2; cf. 13:11–16)

"The firstborn of every living thing, human or animal, presented to the Lord belongs to you. But you must certainly redeem a human firstborn, and redeem the firstborn of an unclean animal. You will pay the redemption price for a month-old male according to your assessment: five shekels of silver by the standard sanctuary shekel, which is twenty gerahs." (Num 18:15–16)

The redemption ("buying back") of the firstborn was a recognition that one's child and livestock belonged to God. Luke's Gentile audience would not have been familiar with these practices, so Luke states these things were done "according to the law of the Lord" (2:24).

Luke next describes the purification of Mary. After a woman gave birth to a child, she was considered ritually unclean. She could perform her household duties, but she could not enter the temple or participate in religious activities (Leviticus 12). At the conclusion of that time, the mother was to bring a lamb to the temple for a burnt offering and a young pigeon for a sin offering. Since the lamb was an expensive offering, the law permitted that in the place of the lamb the woman may offer a second pigeon. The offering of two pigeons instead of a lamb was called "The Offering of the Poor." Due to our unfamiliarity with this practice, the key passage is printed in full.

The Lord spoke to Moses: "Tell the Israelites: When a woman becomes pregnant and gives birth to a male child, she will be unclean seven days, as she is during the days of her menstrual impurity. The flesh of his foreskin must be circumcised on the eighth day. She will continue in purification from her bleeding for thirty-three days. She must not touch any holy thing or go into the sanctuary until completing her days of purification. But if she gives birth to a female child, she will be unclean for two weeks as she is during her menstrual impurity. She will continue in purification from her bleeding for sixty-six days. When her days of purification are complete, whether for a son or daughter, she is to bring to the priest at the entrance to the tent of meeting a year-old male lamb for a burnt offering, and a young pigeon or a turtledove for a sin offering. He will present them before the LORD and make atonement on her behalf; she will be clean from her discharge of blood. This is the law for a woman giving birth, whether to a male or female. But if she doesn't have sufficient means for a sheep, she may take two turtledoves or two young pigeons, one for a burnt offering and the other for a sin offering. Then the priest will make atonement on her behalf, and she will be clean." (Lev 12:1–8)

While one could misunderstand God's isolation of the mother and child to be harsh and capricious, such a time of isolation demonstrates the graciousness and wisdom of God. The time of isolation provides the mother and child with time to recover from childbirth and allows time for their natural immunities to be strengthened before returning to community activities.

The Song of Simeon (2:25–35)

An elderly man now steps out of the darkness of the story line of Scripture and onto the main stage. Bock describes Simeon as "a simple man, a layman, not a priest, who dwells in Jerusalem."[3]

---

[3] Bock, *Luke*, 1:237.

We will examine first who he was and then what he said. Luke describes Simeon's character in terms reminiscent of what he said of Zechariah and Elizabeth. Simeon was righteous, devout, waiting for the consolation of Israel,[4] and the Holy Spirit was at work in his life. The repetition of references to the Spirit is impressive: "the Holy Spirit was on him" (v. 25), "revealed to him by the Holy Spirit" (v. 26), and "guided by the Spirit" (v. 26). The description of Simeon reveals a man with a heart for God—orthodox, godly, and anointed.

We do not know how Simeon was able to recognize Jesus's messianic identity when he saw him, except by divine revelation. Simeon had waited much of his life for this moment. God had promised him he would not die before he had seen the Messiah. Now, in what appears to be the final years of Simeon's life, the promise was fulfilled. In his exuberance, Simeon sang what is known as the *Nunc Dimittis*, meaning "[you] now dismiss" (v. 29).[5] The title of the song indicates Simeon's readiness to die. This song is the last of the four in Luke's Birth and Infancy narrative. Simeon's words bear repeating:

Now, Master,
you can dismiss your servant in peace,
as you promised.
For my eyes have seen your salvation.
You have prepared it

---

[4] Robert H. Stein, *Luke*, vol. 24, The New American Commentary (Nashville: B&H Academic, 1992), 114–15. Stein indicates the phrase "waiting for the consolation of Israel" "refers to the consolation that would be brought about by the inauguration of the messianic age." For more on "the consolation of Israel" see Bock, *Luke*, 1:238.

[5] Bock, *Luke*, 1:241. Bock describes Simeon's words as "prophetic praise."

in the presence of all peoples—
a light for revelation to the Gentiles
and glory to your people Israel. (Luke 2:29–32)

Simeon's words are astonishing. He did not say he was looking at the Messiah, but as he looked at the baby, he saw "your [God's] salvation" (v. 30). His words emphasize that salvation was for all people—Gentiles and Jews (vv. 31–32).

As mentioned earlier, in Genesis 12, God made a covenant with Abraham by which God promised to bless the entire world through Abraham's seed. Genesis 12:2–3 reads, "I will make you into a great nation, I will bless you, I will make your name great, and you will be a blessing. I will bless those who bless you, I will curse anyone who treats you with contempt, and all the peoples on earth will be blessed through you." When God made his covenant with Abraham, God made clear to Abraham that the Jewish nation was to be a blessing to the entire world. Paul made clear that the promises made to Abraham were fulfilled through Jesus Christ (Gal 3:8, 14).[6] The salvation of the Gentiles referenced by Simeon must have meant much to Luke and his Gentile readers. God's plan always involved the salvation of all people. Simeon's words reflect God's promise to Abraham coming to fruition.

Even after all Mary and Joseph had experienced, from angelic revelations to the shepherds' visit, the young couple was still astonished by Simeon's declaration. How could this stranger know these things about their child?[7] After pronouncing a blessing on the family (v. 34a), Simeon's words took an

---

[6] See Garland's helpful discussion of promise and fulfillment in *Luke*, 83–84.

[7] Stein, *Luke*, 116.

unexpected turn (v. 34b). Simeon spoke directly to Mary. Although Simeon's prophecy was not a direct quotation from Isa 8:14–15 and Isa 28:16, the imagery almost certainly comes from these two passages.[8]

> He will be a sanctuary;
> but for the two houses of Israel,
> he will be a stone to stumble over
> and a rock to trip over,
> and a trap and a snare to the inhabitants of Jerusalem.
> Many will stumble over these;
> they will fall and be broken;
> they will be snared and captured. (Isa 8:14–15)

> Therefore the Lord GOD said:
> "Look, I have laid a stone in Zion,
> a tested stone,
> a precious cornerstone, a sure foundation;
> the one who believes will be unshakable." (Isa 28:16)

Simeon's prophecy describes two responses to Jesus among those in Israel. For some, the Messiah will be a stone that caused them to stumble and a rock that made them fall (Isa 8:14); and for others, the Messiah became a precious cornerstone upon which they would rise (Isa 28:16; cf. Ps 118:22).[9] Much as Isaiah's prophecies divided Israel into a faithful remnant and an apostate majority, the sign of Jesus resulted in a similar separation. Luke's Gospel describes the outworking of Simeon's prophecy

---

[8] Stein, *Luke*, 117.

[9] See Garland, *Luke*, 139–40. See Garland's insightful theological reflection, "The Falling and Rising of Many in Israel."

here—Jesus's ministry divides people. For example, in Luke 12:51–53, Jesus quoted Mic 7:6.

"Do you think that I came here to bring peace on the earth? No, I tell you, but rather division. From now on, five in one household will be divided: three against two, and two against three.

They will be divided, father against son,
son against father,
mother against daughter,
daughter against mother,
mother-in-law against her daughter-in-law,
and daughter-in-law against mother-in-law."[10]

While Mary may not have grasped the full import of Simeon's prophecy, she must have been deeply troubled by his words. The image of a sword being thrust into a person is brutal, violent, and terrifying.[11] The most likely understanding was that this was a prophecy concerning the cross. One can only wonder if Mary did not feel that sword pierce her soul as she watched her firstborn son die on Calvary's cross (John 19:25–27).

A couple of observations about Simeon are appropriate here. First, Simeon saw the Savior in a small baby. What captures our hearts, we see with our eyes. Obviously, Simeon was the recipient of divine revelation in his recognition of the baby Jesus, but his heart was in tune with God's Word,

---

[10] Bock, *Luke*, 1:247, sees the following verses in Luke as further substantiating the fact that Jesus's ministry brings division: 4:29; 6:20–49; 13:28–29; 13:33–35; 16:25; 18:9–14; 19:44, 47–48; 20:14–18.

[11] Scholars debate the precise meaning of this imagery. Bock lists ten possibilities in *Luke*, 1:248–250.

which prepared him for this revelation. Second, once again we see promises made and promises kept. In divine providence, the Spirit led Simeon to the temple at just the right time. When one considers the odds of Simeon at the right place at exactly the right moment, the encounter seems impossible. But Simeon's God is the God of the impossible, and God always keeps his promises.

The Prophecy of the Widow Anna (2:36–38)

From an elderly man, Luke shifts attention to an elderly woman. While Simeon and Anna were not married like Zechariah and Elizabeth, they are presented by Luke as a pair. All four of them were in the twilight years of their lives. All four of them lived in a day when the Pharisees had placed heavy burdens on people's lives by their extrabiblical rules and regulations. The spiritual condition of Israel was deplorably low, evidenced by their rejection of God's Son.

Zechariah, Elizabeth, Simeon, Anna, Joseph, and Mary had hearts aflame for God. We live in a day when people are prone to blame anyone and everyone for their own casual approach to following Jesus. Some blame their church or pastor, while others blame their spouse or career. These six individuals are an example that one can live passionately for God despite being surrounded by dead orthodoxy. May God raise up an army of men and women like those we are studying here. What about you? Are you following in their footsteps, or are you making excuses for living a casual form of Christianity?

The name Anna means "gracious." (In Hebrew her name is Hannah.) She is described as a prophetess, a daughter of Phanuel, a widow, and one looking for the redemption of

Jerusalem. Tragically, after only seven years of marriage, Anna's husband died. At eighty-four years of age, she continued to serve God in the temple. When Luke says she never left the temple, he is speaking hyperbolically, unless she lived in one of the rooms adjacent to the temple precinct. More likely, Anna centered her life on serving God at the temple.

Heartbreaking situations like the loss of a loved one can cause a person to become embittered and calloused toward God. One of Satan's diabolical strategies is to attack believers during dark days. People let down their guard during times of suffering. Believers can make very poor decisions during those seasons. Anna, however, was found serving God in his temple. Rather than tragedy pushing her away from God, tragedy seemed to have driven her closer to God.

Anna, along with Elizabeth and Mary, played an important role in the Birth narrative. Luke, more than Matthew and Mark, highlights the key role women played in the ministry of Jesus. We have already noted the significant roles played by Elizabeth, Mary, and Anna, but Luke does not stop there. Luke alone mentions the women who were key financial supporters of Jesus and his disciples (8:2–3). Only Luke tells the story of Mary and Martha (10:38–42). In fact, Mark and Matthew never mention Mary and Martha. Only Luke records Jesus's parable of the unjust judge giving in to an elderly widow's pestering as an example of persistent prayer (18:2–5). Luke is the only evangelist to record Jesus's words to the "Daughters of Jerusalem" as he was being led to the cross (23:27–29). The four Gospels all record the significant role women played in the hours following Jesus's resurrection. Once again, we see the gospel is good news for all people, regardless of their ethnicity, educational background, socioeconomic standing, or gender.

Luke's wording in 2:38, "At that very moment," indicates God's providence. Just as God providentially guided Simeon to the temple at exactly the right time, God placed Anna in just the right place at just the right time. As the shepherds told everyone who would listen about what they learned from the angels and their subsequent encounter with Jesus and his parents, so Anna did much the same, speaking to everyone "looking forward to the redemption of Jerusalem."

The Family's Return to Nazareth (2:39–40)

When Mary and Joseph completed everything required by the law, they returned to Bethlehem. As mentioned earlier, Luke does not refer to the coming of the magi or the journey to Egypt (Matt 2:1–23). We don't know where Mary and Joseph and Jesus lived during their extended stay in Bethlehem. The beauty of the fourfold Gospel witness is how the four Gospels provide a fuller picture of Christ's life. Matthew's and Luke's accounts are not contradictory but complementary. We know from Matthew's Gospel that Joseph led his family to and from Egypt, and eventually they returned to Nazareth. Luke concludes this section with a brief statement on Jesus's development: "The boy grew up and became strong, filled with wisdom, and God's grace was on him" (v. 40). Jesus was both God and man. Those who watched him grow saw him develop much as every boy his age developed.

Final Reflections

Once again, we find in this passage rich insights for Christian faith and practice. First, Joseph and Mary are presented as young parents doing family life well. They were not a perfect couple or perfect parents, but their obedience to God's Word is impressive. The offering of the two pigeons reveals they were not a well-to-do couple, but that did not prevent them from presenting offerings to God. Children are a gift from the Lord, and godly parenting requires an investment of one's life in raising children for God's glory. One of a parent's greatest challenges is seeing their children's spiritual lives as ultimately more important than their children's athletic pursuits and academic successes. Of course, nothing is inherently wrong with athletics and academics, but far too many Christian parents are willing to sacrifice their child's spiritual life for the good, while missing the best. Mary and Joseph are depicted as a couple that put first things first. Their obedience to the fulfillment of ancient ceremonies reveals a young couple deeply devoted to God and caring for their son in a God-honoring way. Every parent should reflect on the example of Joseph and Mary and redouble their own efforts to raise their children in a manner that prioritizes worship and service to God.

Second, ceremonies matter. The first few verses of this section focus on three ceremonies, which seem odd to twenty-first century Christians, but these ceremonies were reminders to God's people of what was important. While circumcision is not a requirement of the New Covenant nor are offerings for the redemption of the firstborn or purification of women after giving birth, there are practices in the church that remind us of what is important. For example, many churches have parent dedication services rather than child dedication services. Infants cannot dedicate themselves to anything, but churches can call parents to stand with their young babies in their arms before their fellow church members and commit themselves to raising their children in the nurture and admonition of the Lord. A pastor leading a congregational prayer for these young parents and for the future salvation of their children can be spiritually meaningful to the parents and the entire church. When baptism and the Lord's Supper are done with an appropriate focus, they become spiritually enriching to those participating. Congregational continuity can be built through the regular practice of meaningful ceremonies.

Third, why did Luke focus on the fulfillment of God's law in this passage? One reason is to show that Jesus's parents were fully devoted to God. More important, to show that even as a baby, Jesus's life fulfilled God's law. The apostle Paul wrote in Gal 4:4–5: "When the time came to completion, God sent his Son, born of a woman, born under the law, to redeem those under the law, so that we might receive adoption as sons." Jesus was born into a Jewish family, and even as a child, Jesus lived in obedience to God's law. In fact, living in obedience to God's law was a requirement for him to be an all-sufficient Savior. Although Jesus was fully human (born of a woman), he never sinned. Therefore, those who put their faith in Jesus as their wrath-bearing substitute become sons and daughters of God.

Finally, Simeon described God's salvation as a "light for revelation to the Gentiles" (v. 32). Light is an image we explored earlier in John's prologue, but it is one worth considering again. The Gentile world was shrouded in moral and spiritual darkness when Jesus came. Paul puts into words their dire spiritual condition,

"So, then, remember that at one time you were Gentiles in the flesh—called 'the uncircumcised' by those called 'the circumcised,' which is done in the flesh by human hands. At that time, you were without Christ, excluded from the citizenship of Israel, and foreigners to the covenants of promise, without hope and without God in the world. But now in Christ Jesus, you who were far away have been brought near by the blood of Christ" (Eph 2:11–13). Simeon speaks of the Savior baby as a "light to the Gentiles." God's plan has always included the entire world of humanity. God intended Israel to be a light to the nations: "I am the LORD. I have called you for a righteous purpose, and I will hold you by your hand. I will watch over you, and I will appoint you to be a covenant for the people and a light to the nations, in order to open blind eyes, to bring out prisoners from the dungeon, and those sitting in darkness from the prison house" (Isa 42:6–7). Where Israel failed, Jesus will succeed as the Light of the World.

A Christmas Hymn of Response

Away in a manger, no crib for a bed,
The little Lord Jesus laid down His sweet head;
The stars in the sky looked down where He lay,
The little Lord Jesus, asleep on the hay.

The cattle are lowing, the Baby awakes,
But little Lord Jesus, no crying He makes;
I love Thee, Lord Jesus! Look down from the sky,
And stay by my cradle till morning is nigh.

Be near me, Lord Jesus, I ask Thee to stay
Close by me forever, and love me, I pray;
Bless all the dear children in Thy tender care,
And fit us for heaven to live with Thee there.[12]

---

[12] William J. Kirkpatrick, "Away in a Manger," 1852, *Baptist Hymnal*, #103.

Taking a Deeper Dive:
The Holy Spirit in Luke's Gospel

Among the Synoptic Gospels, Luke's emphasis on the Spirit (seventeen times) far exceeds Mark's (six times) and Matthew's (twelve times).[13] As we have seen, the Holy Spirit played a significant role in Luke's Birth and Infancy narrative. Gabriel informed Zechariah that John would be filled with the Holy Spirit while still in Elizabeth's womb (1:15). In addition, John would go before the Lord ministering in the spirit and power of Elijah (1:17). Whether the word "spirit" should be capitalized here or not is debated; clearly the Holy Spirit and power are often associated in Luke and Acts (e.g., Luke 1:35; 4:14; Acts 1:8; 10:38). The age of the Spirit was beginning with the ministry of Jesus's forerunner, John the Baptist.

The virginal conception was the result of the powerful working of the Holy Spirit (1:35). In response to Mary's question as to how she could conceive a child while not having consummated her marriage to Joseph, Gabriel replied, "The Holy Spirit will come upon you, and the power of the Most High will overshadow you. Therefore, the holy one to be born will be called the Son of God" (1:35). A short time later, when Elizabeth heard Mary's greeting, she was filled with the Spirit and prophesied (1:41). At the birth of John, when Zechariah affirmed the baby's name, he was filled with the Holy Spirit and prophesied (1:67).

When Simeon encountered Jesus at the temple, the Spirit had been at work in his life for quite some time. Luke recounts how the Spirit was on Simeon and revealed to him that he would not die before he saw the Messiah. The Spirit then led Simeon

---

[13] Stein, *Luke*, 47.

into the temple at the very time Mary and Joseph had taken Jesus into the temple (2:25–27).

When Jesus entered the wilderness to confront Satan, he was "full of the Holy Spirit" and "led by the Spirit" (4:1). Of the Synoptics, only Luke has a twofold reference to the Spirit here. Jesus came out of the wilderness in the power of the Spirit (4:14). Again, this verse is unique to Luke. For Luke to say Jesus was led by the Spirit into the wilderness is to say that Jesus was not ambushed by Satan. Rather, Jesus, under the leadership of the Spirit, took the battle to the devil. To describe Jesus as being filled with the Spirit prepares the way for the Spirit's fullness in God's people in the book of Acts. Jesus came out of the wilderness and began his ministry in "the power of the Spirit" (4:14). He entered the wilderness led by the Spirit and full of the Spirit, and he came out of the wilderness after his encounter in the power of the Spirit. While it is possible to make too much of this statement, the implication is that the Spirit's power in ministry is reserved for those who defeat the devil in combat by refusing to succumb to his temptations.

The age of the Spirit dawned in a new way with the coming of the Son of God. Paul commanded the church at Ephesus "to be filled with the Spirit" (Eph 5:18 NIV). Those who walk by the Spirit manifest the fruit of the Spirit (Gal 5:22). The "sword of the Spirit" is the Word of God and is a reliable weapon to fend off the attacks of the enemy (Eph 6:17).

CHAPTER 11

THE WORSHIP OF
THE NATIONS

MATTHEW 2:1–12

> "Where is he who has been born king of
> the Jews? For we saw his star at its rising
> and have come to worship him."
> —Matthew 2:2

Christmas is God's yearly invitation for seekers to contemplate the true meaning of Jesus's coming, the true meaning of Christmas. While Jesus's birth was a well-kept secret, God whispered his Son's arrival among the stars for those with eyes to see. While only a handful of Jewish people knew what had transpired in Bethlehem—Mary and Joseph, a group of shepherds, Simeon, and Anna—approximately eight hundred miles away, a group of uncircumcised Gentiles saw a star and recognized its significance. What a strange turn of events for the Jewish Messiah to be recognized by foreigners, and of all people—astrologers. How strange that the announcement of the arrival of the Messiah's star was not made to Jewish priests or the

Sanhedrin. How odd that the message came to wise men (*magos*), sometimes called magi, rather than to the Jewish Sanhedrin.

Why did Matthew include this story? Both Matthew and Luke were more than just historians, they were theologians as well.[1] As theologians, they chose their stories carefully and told them with intentionality. Therefore, we need to ask, what is Matthew's purpose in recounting this story? What is Matthew teaching us about Jesus, and how do the characters in the story respond to Jesus?

One of the main theological points in the entirety of Matthew 2 is how the places Jesus lived—Bethlehem, Egypt, and Nazareth—fulfilled the Scriptures. Ancient prophecies were being fulfilled in meticulous fashion. In this specific story, Jesus's kingship is contrasted with Herod's kingship.[2] Jesus is the true "king of the Jews," while Herod was an imposter. Furthermore, the wise men's arduous journey in seeking for the king is to be contrasted with Herod's hostility and the religious leadership's apathy.

Wise Men from the East (2:1–3)

The wise men's visit is one of the most beloved episodes of the Christmas story. A favorite Christmas hymn reflecting on this

---

[1] The historicity of the pericope has been subject to intense scrutiny over the last century. The following scholars argue successfully for accepting the event's historicity: D. A. Carson, "Matthew," in *Matthew and Mark*, ed. Tremper Longman III and David E. Garland, The Expositor's Bible Commentary (Grand Rapids: Zondervan, 2010), 107–8. Grant R. Osborne, *Matthew*, Zondervan Exegetical Commentary on the New Testament (Grand Rapids: Zondervan, 2010), 85.

[2] Ben Witherington III, *Matthew*, Smyth & Helwys Bible Commentary (Macon, GA: Smyth & Helwys, 2006), 57.

event is John Henry Hopkins's "We Three Kings." This beautiful Christmas Carol, however, has two historical inaccuracies. First, Matthew does not tell us how many wise men worshiped Jesus. Many think that since three gifts are mentioned, there must have been three wise men. As the tradition developed, the three "kings" were given the names Balthasar, Melchior, and Caspar, but they were never described as kings.[3] Another misunderstanding is often found in nativity sets depicting the wise men at the stable along with the shepherds. While the shepherds visited the baby Jesus on the night of his birth, the wise men came approximately two years later. When the wise men arrived, the family was residing in a house and not a stable (v. 11), and Jesus is referred to as a child and not a baby (v. 8).

The story of the coming of the wise men is unique to Matthew's Gospel. If we were only to read Matthew, we might get the impression that Joseph and Mary's original hometown was Bethlehem and not Nazareth. Matthew does not mention the journey from Nazareth to Bethlehem, as Luke does. We likely should assume Matthew's readers were familiar with Joseph and Mary's hometown being Nazareth rather than Bethlehem, since they return to Nazareth after their sojourn in Egypt.

Although the wise men were not kings, the story does have two kings. The first king was a charlatan—Herod the Great. As we have noted earlier, Herod the Great ruled the Jewish people from 37 BC until his death in 4 BC. Herod was Idumean by birth. Despite being a brutal dictator, he was also known as a

---

[3] Craig L. Blomberg, *Matthew*, vol. 22, The New American Commentary (Nashville: Broadman, 1992), 66 n. 31. Carson traces this tradition to Tertullian in the second century; see Carson, "Matthew," 110.

builder.[4] Herod's most famous project was the beautification and expansion of the Jerusalem temple. In addition, he built a palace at Jericho; the harbor city of Caesarea Maritima; and fortresses such as Machaerus on the eastern shore of the Dead Sea, Sebaste in Samaria, Masada in the Judean wilderness, and the Herodium in Jerusalem. While Jesus built no palaces or fortresses, the magi worship him as the true "King of the Jews."

The precise identity of the wise men is disputed. Many scholars speculate that the wise men (magi) came from Babylon or Persia. Michael Wilkins notes, "These Magi were leading figures in the religious court life of their country of origin, employing a variety of scientific (astrology), diplomacy (wisdom), and religious (magical incantations) means to understand present and future life."[5] Their exposure to Judaism would have been with Jews who did not return to Israel after the exile. If the wise men came from Babylon, they traveled approximately eight hundred miles. If they traveled twenty to twenty-five miles per day, then their journey would have taken thirty to forty days. They would have needed a substantial food and water supply to travel for this great distance. All of this may explain the lengthy time between Jesus's birth and the arrival of the wise men. Furthermore, they would have needed to travel with at least a small caravan for protection from bandits.

These wise men would have left behind their families and homes to make the journey. They would have experienced the terrible heat by day and the frigid cold by night. If they were

---

[4] Helen Bond, "Herodian Dynasty," in *Dictionary of Jesus and the Gospels*, ed. Joel B. Green, 2nd ed. (Downers Grove: IVP Academic, 2013), 379–82.

[5] Michael Wilkins, *Matthew*, The Zondervan Illustrated Bible Backgrounds Commentary (Grand Rapids: Zondervan, 2011), 13–14.

The Worship of the Nations

guided primarily by the star, much of their journey would have taken place at night. These wise men demonstrated a tenacity that would not be satisfied until they found the one for whom they searched. The wise men are reminiscent of Jer 29:13, "You will seek me and find me when you search for me with all your heart." Jesus does not give himself away to the casual comer and goer. Jesus is found by those who seek him wholeheartedly, as illustrated by the wise men.

Throughout Matthew's Birth narrative, divine guidance is communicated through angels and dreams (1:20; 2:12, 13, 19, 22), and now by a star (2:2). The identification of the star is a great mystery. The wise men report to Herod that they saw his star "at its rising" ("when it rose," NIV) which is a better translation than the traditional "in the east" because the wise men from the east would have seen the star in the west. The star's movement suggests it was not a natural phenomenon such as a comet, planetary conjunction, or a supernova. The star was likely a miraculous creation by God to guide the wise men to their desired destination.[6] Whatever the star's identity, these magi from the east were convinced that a great king had been born. The wise men may have been familiar with Balaam's prophecy in Num 24:17, "I see him, but not now; I perceive him, but not near. A star will come from Jacob, and a scepter will arise from Israel."[7] Once again, the wise men would have learned of this prophecy from Jewish exiles.

---

[6] See the discussions on the star's identification in Michael J. Wilkins, *Matthew*, NIV Application Commentary (Grand Rapids: Zondervan, 2004), 95–96; Osborne, *Matthew*, 87.

[7] Similar language is used of Jesus in Luke 1:78; 2 Pet 1:19; Rev 22:16. Jesus speaks of himself in similar language in Rev 22:16 when he says, "I am the Root and descendant of David, the bright morning star."

Where Was the Messiah to Be Born? (2:3–6)

The wise men followed the star to Jerusalem, possibly thinking the king of the Jews would be born there. Their inquiry troubled *(tarassō)* Herod greatly. The word translated "trouble" is not quite strong enough to describe Herod's response. The news of a rival king's birth terrified him. He was never fully accepted as king by the Jewish people because of his Idumean lineage. Herod's lack of scriptural knowledge is evident when he turns to the religious leaders to learn where the Messiah was to be born. Matthew indicates that "all Jerusalem" was disturbed as well. The probable reason for the widespread concerns of the citizens of Jerusalem was their knowledge of Herod's brutality and desire to demolish any threat to his throne.[8]

Herod sought the answer from the chief priests and teachers of the law (scribes) (v. 4). The chief priests oversaw the activities of the temple and came from the sect of the Sadducees. The scribes were responsible for the interpretation and application of the law and aligned themselves primarily with the sect of the Pharisees. The Sadducees and Pharisees were very different from each other in theology and religious practices. The Sadducees believed that the Pentateuch (the first five books of the Old Testament) held a place of greater authority than the rest of the Scriptures. The Pharisees gave equal authority to the Pentateuch, Prophets, and Writings. The Sadducees controlled the temple; therefore, their base of authority was in Jerusalem. The Pharisees and the teachers of the law had greater sway in the synagogues and were more popular among the people. Unlike the Pharisees, the Sadducees rejected the oral traditions, while the Pharisees

---

[8] Osborne, *Matthew*, 88.

understood them to be equally authoritative to the law. Although the two sects despised one another, they would eventually come together to hand Jesus over to the Romans for execution.[9]

The religious leaders pointed to Mic 5:2 to answer the wise men's question (vv. 5–6). Seven hundred years earlier, Micah prophesied of the Messiah's birth in Bethlehem. Matthew adds the words "are by no means" to the prophecy, not as a contradiction to Micah but to reflect the fact that this small village will no longer be insignificant "among the rulers of Judah," as it once had been.[10] Bethlehem would now be forever famous as the Messiah's birthplace. The second part of the quotation may reference 2 Sam 5:2 ("who will shepherd my people Israel"), teaching that the coming Messiah would be the shepherd of God's people.

The Wise Men's Journey Is Rewarded (2:7–12)

Herod asked the magi about the precise time the star appeared to them (v. 7). This information enabled Herod to infer the general age of the child. Before dispatching the wise men, Herod secretly requested they bring him information concerning the location of the newborn king. He did this under the guise that he desired to worship this newborn king as well (v. 8).

What a striking contrast between the Gentile seekers and Herod. Although Herod seemed to believe the wise men's report, he did not bother to travel the short distance to Bethlehem to confirm

---

[9] For a more complete discussion on the Pharisees, see Lynn H. Cohick, "Pharisees," in *Dictionary of Jesus and the Gospels*, ed. Joel B. Green, 2nd ed. (Downers Grove: IVP Academic, 2013), 673–79. On the Sadducees see Mark L. Strauss, "Sadducees," 823–25, in the same volume.

[10] For further discussion, see Carson, "Matthew," 114–15.

their story. What is even more shocking is the religious leaders' seeming indifference in traveling to Bethlehem themselves. As the wise men resumed their journey, the star suddenly reappeared to them and led them to Bethlehem and stopped over the place where Jesus and his family lived (vv. 9–10). After weeks of traveling, their journey was complete. These sojourners must have been shocked to discover the child was not living in a palace but likely in a typical one-room home. What a strange dwelling for a king.

The wise men fell to their knees in worship for the King of the Jews.[11] They presented expensive gifts to the young king (v. 11). These gifts would probably fund the family's future flight to Egypt (cf. 2:13–23). Some have understood these gifts as symbolic of Jesus's identity and future work.[12] If this is the case, then gold was a gift for a king: "May he live long! May gold from Sheba be given to him. May prayer be offered for him continually, and may he be blessed all day long" (Ps 72:15). Frankincense was a fragrance obtained from the bark of trees and was a gift for deity: "Caravans of camels will cover your land—young camels of Midian and Ephah—all of them will come from Sheba. They will carry gold and frankincense and proclaim the praises of the LORD" (Isa 60:6). Frankincense was used ceremonially to burn on the altar (Exod 30:34–38). Myrrh was a valued spice used in burials: "Nicodemus [who had previously come to him at night] also came, bringing a mixture of about seventy-five pounds of myrrh and aloes. They took Jesus's body and wrapped it in linen cloths with the fragrant spices, according to the burial custom of

---

[11] Craig S. Keener, *A Commentary on the Gospel of Matthew* (Grand Rapids: Zondervan, 2002), 103–4.

[12] Carson traces this tradition to Tertullian in the second century, Carson, "Matthew," 110.

the Jews" (John 19:39–40). Whether Matthew intended the gifts to be understood symbolically is impossible to know for certain since he does not specifically ascribe symbolic significance to the gifts. A better allusion may be to Isaiah 60, with the picture of a day when foreigners will come to Jerusalem:

> "Arise, shine, for your light has come,
> and the glory of the LORD shines over you.
> For look, darkness will cover the earth,
> And total darkness the peoples;
> but the LORD will shine over you,
> and his glory will appear over you.
> Nations will come to your light,
> and kings to your shining brightness.
> Raise your eyes and look around:
> they all gather and come to you;
> your sons will come from far away,
> and your daughters on the hips of nursing mothers.
> Then you will see and be radiant,
> and your heart will tremble and rejoice,
> because the riches of the sea will become yours
> and the wealth of the nations will come to you.
> Caravans of camels will cover your land—
> young camels of Midian and Ephah—
> all of them will come from Sheba.
> They will carry gold and frankincense
> and proclaim the praises of the LORD.
> All the flocks of Kedar will be gathered to you;
> the rams of Nebaioth will serve you
> and go up on my altar as an acceptable sacrifice.
> I will glorify my beautiful house." (Isa 60:1–7)

The wise men's adoration of Jesus is impressive. Their actions are reported with great specificity: they entered the home, they bowed before him, they gave him expensive gifts, and they worshiped him. After being warned by God in a dream not to return to Herod, they returned home by a different route, thereby avoiding Herod's scrutiny for a time (v. 12). The magi's dream to avoid Herod was another demonstration of God's providential care for his Son.

Final Reflections

The thought that Christianity is not an ethnic religion could not be made any clearer than by the coming of the wise men. The wise men were the forerunners of the Gentiles who will come to worship Jesus as Savior and Lord. This story is found only in Matthew's Gospel, the most Jewish of the four Gospels. Even though Matthew's Gospel is the most Jewish, it contains some wonderful indications that reveal Jesus's love for Gentiles. We have already read the names of Gentile women in Jesus's genealogy—Rahab and Ruth. As Jesus launches his Galilean ministry, Matthew quotes Isa 9:1–2 to demonstrate Jesus's intention to include the Gentiles in his saving work. The important passage from Isaiah reads, "Land of Zebulun and land of Naphtali, along the road by the sea, beyond the Jordan, Galilee of the Gentiles. The people who live in darkness have seen a great light, and for those living in the land of the shadow of death, a light has dawned" (Matt 4:15–16). After Jesus heals a Roman centurion's servant, he speaks of a time when from the east, west, north, and south people will come and eat with "Abraham, Isaac, and Jacob in the kingdom of heaven" (Matt 8:11). In the parable of the wheat and the tares, the field where the farmer (Jesus) sows his seed (the sons of the kingdom) is the world (Matt 13:36–43). Jesus scatters his people throughout the world for the salvation of all people. Matthew concludes with the famous Great Commission, where Jesus's followers are to go and make disciples of all nations (Matt 28:16–20). These passages remind us that Christ's coming is a call to worldwide missions—across the street and around the world. No one truly grasps the significance of Jesus's coming without embracing his call to evangelism. Christianity is not an ethnic religion but a faith to be embraced by every race and nationality.

While Matthew has a unique focus on the wise men, Luke is focused on the shepherds. Both the wise men and the shepherds worshiped Jesus. The two groups, however, could not have been more different. First, there was the ethnic difference. The magi were Gentiles, and the shepherds were Jewish. Second, while the shepherds likely had little formal education beyond the synagogue, the wise men received an excellent education in Babylon or Persia. Third, the economic difference would have been noticeable as well. The wise men brought Jesus expensive gifts, while the shepherds brought only the report of the angel's words. The shepherds represent the worship of the "have-nots" of the world, while the wise men represent the worship of the more well-to-do. This universal appeal of Jesus Christ drew shepherds from their flocks and wise men from the East. They both had the goal of finding the King of the Jews and worshiping him.

Worship is an important theme in this passage (vv. 2, 8). While Herod expressed a desire to worship Jesus under false pretenses, the wise men desired to worship him with sincere hearts. The wise men's worship demonstrated great personal sacrifice. They traveled hundreds of miles searching for the King of the Jews. They brought expensive gifts as an expression of

their worship of him. As they prepared to leave Jerusalem and
the star returned, they were filled with joy. Joy is a characteristic
experience of those who worship the King. When warned in a
dream not to return to Herod, the magi demonstrate obedience
to God in the face of enraging Herod. The wise men teach us
that Christmas is not only about worldwide missions but heartfelt sacrificial worship.

In comparison to the response of the wise men, Herod's
response to the news of the Messiah's birth was rage, as evidenced in the murder of the babies (2:16–18). The religious leaders' response to the news of the Messiah's birth was unbelievable
apathy. Although they had waited for centuries for the Messiah's
arrival, they would not even journey to Bethlehem to verify the
wise men's report. The religious leaders knew where the Messiah
would be born, but they had no interest in discovering the truth
about his birth. Scriptural knowledge without heart devotion does
not help very much. Although many people in churches today
know the answers to important theological questions, their knowledge of Scripture does not move their hearts in loving devotion
and obedience to Jesus. Knowing about Jesus and having a life-
transforming encounter with him are not the same thing.

Once again, we are faced with the question upon which
every person's destiny is determined: "Who do you believe Jesus
Christ to be?" You may be a seeker, like the magi. If you seek
him with all your heart, you will find him (Jer 29:13). Or you
may be much like Herod, holding on tenaciously to your own
little kingdom rather than falling before Jesus and worshiping
him. You may be more like the religious teachers, having all the
right answers in your head but your heart is too apathetic to give
him the treasures of your life. The wise men teach us that the
only appropriate response to King Jesus is to bow before him

in worship. The greatest gift that we can give him is our lives in devotion and service.

A Christmas Hymn of Response

We three kings of Orient are
Bearing gifts we traverse afar—
Field and fountain, moor and mountain—
Following yonder star.

O star of wonder, star of night,
Star with royal beauty bright,
Westward leading, still proceeding,
Guide us to thy perfect light.

Born a king on Bethlehem's plain:
Gold I bring to crown Him again,
King forever, ceasing never,
Over us all to reign.

O star of wonder, star of night,
Star with royal beauty bright,
Westward leading, still proceeding,
Guide us to thy perfect light.

Frankincense to offer have I,
Incense owns a Deity nigh;
Prayer and praising, all men raising,
Worship Him, God on high.

O star of wonder, star of night,
Star with royal beauty bright,
Westward leading, still proceeding,
Guide us to thy perfect light.

Myrrh is mine, Its bitter perfume
Breathes a life of gathering gloom—
Sorr'wing, sighing, bleeding, dying,
Sealed in the stone-cold tomb.

O star of wonder, star of night,
Star with royal beauty bright,
Westward leading, still proceeding,
Guide us to thy perfect light.

Glorious now behold Him arise:
King and God and Sacrifice;
Alleluia, Alleluia!
Earth to heav'n replies.

O star of wonder, star of night,
Star with royal beauty bright,
Westward leading, still proceeding,
Guide us to thy perfect light.[13]

---

[13] John Henry Hopkins, Jr., "We Three Kings of Orient Are," 1857, *Baptist Hymnal*, #113.

CHAPTER 12

THE FLIGHT TO EGYPT AND RETURN

(*MATTHEW 2:13–23*)

> "A voice was heard in Ramah,
> weeping, and great mourning,
> Rachel weeping for her children;
> and she refused to be consoled,
> because they are no more."
> —Matthew 2:18

A few years after Joseph and Mary settled into their new home in Bethlehem, one of the most horrific events recorded in the Bible transpired—"the Murder of the Innocents." This appalling massacre is, understandably, never portrayed in church Christmas pageants. Matthew alone recounts Herod's slaughter of the baby boys in and around Bethlehem. God the Father, however, rescued his beloved Son by warning Joseph in a dream to flee to Egypt. This passage continues the Matthean theme that the locations where Jesus lived—Bethlehem, Egypt, and Nazareth—were foretold by the prophets.

A Nighttime Escape to Egypt (2:13–15)

Matthew suggests that the family decided to remain in Bethlehem after Jesus's birth. A possible reason was to escape the scandal back in Nazareth. Joseph's skills would have enabled him to find work, and the family could settle into a peaceful routine. Yet the coming of the Light into the world meant the darkness would try and extinguish the Light. Matthew describes Herod's attempt to do just that by the killing of the baby boys in the village of Bethlehem.

When Herod realized the wise men tricked him by returning home a different way, he must have gone into a violent rage. Shortly before the arrival of Herod's soldiers in Bethlehem, an angel warned Joseph in a dream to leave Bethlehem immediately. The angel specifically instructed Joseph to take his family to Egypt, where Jesus would be safe from Herod's murderous plot (v. 13). Just as Joseph responded promptly when told to take Mary as his wife, he did so once again by wasting no time in obeying the angel's instructions. Time was of the essence, and the family left in the middle of the night.

The distance from Bethlehem to the border of Egypt was approximately ninety miles. The gifts from the wise men would enable the family to travel to Egypt and eventually return to Nazareth. In the first century, Egypt was a Roman province outside Herod's jurisdiction. The country presented a natural hiding place for the family since many dispersed Jewish people lived there.[1] As long ago as the time of Abraham, Egypt had been

---

[1] D. A. Carson, "Matthew," in *Matthew and Mark*, ed. Tremper Longman III and David E. Garland, The Expositor's Bible Commentary (Grand Rapids: Zondervan, 2010), 90.

a haven for the Hebrew people during difficult periods (Gen 12:10; 1 Kgs 11:40; Jer 26:21). A significant Jewish community resided in Alexandria, Egypt, if the family chose to travel that far. Wilkins suggests that if the family traveled the primary route from Bethlehem to Egypt, they would journey south to Hebron. [2] From Hebron, they would travel west to Gaza and then turn south again to the border of the Nabateans. From there, the journey is approximately fifty miles to the Egyptian border, but still another two hundred miles to Alexandria. The family remained in Egypt until Herod's death in 4 BC. If Jesus was born in approximately 7 or 6 BC and the wise men arrived around the time Jesus turned two years of age, then the family's sojourn in Egypt would not have lasted long.

Matthew understood the family's return from Egypt to fulfill Hos 11:1, "Out of Egypt I called my son." How is Matthew's quotation of Hos 11:1 to be understood? Once again, at first glance, Matthew's use of this Old Testament text does not appear appropriate. We should not, however, assume that Matthew simply chose Hos 11:1 out of thin air. Instead, Matthew compared the events of Jesus's life to the Old Testament, and he saw a pattern. In Matt 2:13, the pattern is one of God calling his beloved son out of Egypt. In many ways Israel (and Moses) is a type of Christ, and Jesus is the anti-type. This can be seen in the fact that God called Israel his son, just as he does Jesus. As Moses led God's son (Israel) out of Egyptian bondage, so Jesus (as a greater Moses and a more faithful son) brings about a new exodus for the sons and daughters of God from slavery to Satan, sin, and death. In his Gospel, Matthew highlights ways Jesus

---

[2] Michael J. Wilkins, *Matthew*, Zondervan Illustrated Bible Backgrounds Commentary (Grand Rapids: Zondervan, 2002), 17.

repeats Israel's history. A clear example is Jesus's wandering in
the wilderness for forty days and overcoming Satan's temptations, while Israel wandered in the wilderness for forty years and
repeatedly fell to temptation. Therefore, it was not a struggle for
Matthew to understand Hos 11:1 as another example of Jesus
retracing Israel's steps. In Hosea's original context, the prophet
recalled how God, through Moses, led Israel out of Egypt. But
as Matthew reflected on Hos 11:1 and the exodus event, he saw
an analogous pattern between Israel's exodus from Egypt and
Jesus's return from Egypt. God considered Israel to be his firstborn son (Exod 4:22–23). Jesus's return from Egypt and Israel's
exodus both demonstrate God at work saving his sons.

    Similarly, John Stott stated:

> As Israel was oppressed in Egypt under the despotic
> rule of pharaoh, so the infant Jesus became a refugee in
> Egypt under the despotic rule of Herod. As Israel passed
> through the waters of the Red Sea, so Jesus passed
> through the waters of John's baptism in the Jordan river.
> As Israel was tested in the wilderness of Zin for 40 years,
> so Jesus was tested in the wilderness of Judea for 40 days.
> And as Moses from Mount Sinai gave Israel the law, so
> Jesus from the Mount of Beatitudes gave his disciples
> the true interpretation and amplification of the law.[3]

    The annual Jewish celebration of Passover commemorates
God's rescue of his people from Egypt by the death of a sacrificial
lamb. In Jesus's day, God was at work in providing a greater exodus, not from Egyptian bondage to Pharaoh's demagoguery but

[3] John Stott, *Through the Bible, Through the Year* (Grand Rapids: Baker
Books, 2006), 154.

from Satan, sin, and death. While the first exodus required each family to kill a spotless lamb, the greater exodus was accomplished by the death of Jesus, the spotless "Lamb of God" (John 1:29; 1 Pet 1:18–20). Rudolph Schnackenberg understands Matthew's use to mean that "the old Mosaic exodus is repeated and fulfilled in a new way. But it's not just that Jesus is like Moses, a new and better deliverer. Rather, Jesus is the embodiment of Israel itself, a new and better 'son.'"[4]

The Massacre of the Innocents (2:16–19)

Herod's violent temper and paranoia were on full display when he ordered his troops to kill the baby boys two years of age and younger in the vicinity of Bethlehem (v. 16).[5] We do not know how many little boys were killed, but regardless of the number, the murderous act was a tragedy. Ezra 2:21 states that only 123 men returned to Bethlehem from the Babylonian exile. Bethlehem appears to have been a small village in Jesus's day with a population of approximately 1,000 people.[6] Although this event is not recounted outside Matthew's Gospel, it conforms perfectly to Herod's character.[7] Craig Keener provides the fol-

---

[4] Rudolf Schnackenburg, *The Gospel of Matthew*, trans. Robert R. Barr (Grand Rapids: Eerdmans, 2002), 27. For a discussion on Old Testament fulfillment in the New Testament and how New Testament authors use Old Testament texts, see Carson, "Matthew," 118–20.

[5] Carson, "Matthew," 94, estimates Jesus's age being between six and twenty months.

[6] Wilkins, *Matthew*, ZIBC, 19.

[7] Some scholars question this story since no extrabiblical evidence corroborates it. In response, see R. T. France, "Herod and the Children of Bethlehem," *NovT* 21 (1979): 98–120. D. A. Carson notes, "That there is no extra-Christian confirmation is not surprising . . . The death of a few

lowing examples of Herod's brutality. During Herod's reign a young, popular high priest "drowned" in a pool only a few feet deep, Herod had his *favorite* wife strangled, he had several of his sons executed, and he ordered numerous significant Jewish people to be executed when he died.[8]

Matthew understood the slaughter of the children to fulfill typologically Jer 31:15: "A voice was heard in Ramah, weeping, and great mourning, Rachel weeping for her children; and she refused to be consoled, because they are no more" (v. 18). For Jeremiah, Rachel symbolized the bereaved mothers in Israel who lost a child in the Babylonian invasion and exile. Rachel was the wife of the patriarch Jacob. When she and Jacob were traveling from Bethel to Bethlehem, they stopped near Ramah for her to give birth to their second son, Benjamin. "During her difficult labor, the midwife said to her, 'Don't be afraid, for you have another son.' With her last breath—for she was dying—she named him Ben-oni, but his father called him Benjamin. So, Rachel died and was buried on the way to Ephrath (that is, Bethlehem). Jacob set up a marker on her grave; it is the marker at Rachel's grave still today" (Gen 35:17–20). At some point during the Babylonian exile, Jeremiah and many others were held prisoners at Ramah (Jer 40:1). The people of God who were taken into exile marched

---

children (perhaps a dozen or so; Bethlehem's total population was not large) would hardly have been recorded in such violent times." Carson, "Matthew," 121. See also Grant R. Osborne, *Matthew*, Zondervan Exegetical Commentary on the New Testament (Grand Rapids: Zondervan, 2010), 99. See Josephus for a discussion of Herod the Great's reign as well as his sons in Cleon L. Rogers Jr., *The Topical Josephus: Historical Accounts That Shed Light on the Bible* (Grand Rapids: Zondervan, 1992), 17–61.

[8] Craig S. Keener, *The IVP Bible Background Commentary: New Testament* (Downers Grove: IVP Academic, 1993), 50.

through Ramah and likely passed near Rachel's tomb. Jeremiah envisioned Rachel metaphorically sobbing in her tomb as the captives passed by on their way to Babylon.

What does Jeremiah 31 have to do with Jesus? The spiritual exile of God's people is coming to an end with Jesus's birth and his own return from exile in Egypt. The verses following Jer 31:15 include God's promised restoration of his people from exile. Jeremiah reads, "This is what the LORD says: Keep your voice from weeping and your eyes from tears, for the reward for your work will come—this is the LORD's declaration—and your children will return from the enemy's land. There is hope for your future—this is the LORD's declaration—and your children will return from the enemy's land" (Jer 31:16). Did you catch the words immediately following Jer 31:15? "Keep your voice from weeping and your eyes from tears." Why would God's people, after being carried off into exile, have any reason for ceasing their tears? The reason they could stop weeping was because Jesus's return from his Egyptian exile pointed toward an even greater return from exile for God's people through Jesus's life and ministry. The people's exile was coming to an end, the people of God will have a new king (Jesus), and they will live under a new covenant (Jer 31:33–34). This is not Matthew's first mention of the end of exile. The first hint comes in Matt 1:17, "So all the generations from Abraham to David were fourteen generations; and from David until the exile to Babylon, fourteen generations; and from the exile to Babylon until the Messiah, fourteen generations." The words of John the apostle in Rev 21:4 capture the moment well, "He will wipe away every tear from their eyes. Death will be no more; grief, crying, and pain will be no more, because the previous things have passed away." What a glorious day that will be!

The Return to Nazareth (2:20–23)

The final section of Matthew's Birth and Infancy narrative focuses again on ancient prophecy being fulfilled. Just as Jesus's being born in Bethlehem and then taken to Egypt and back fulfilled Old Testament prophecies, so does the fact Jesus will be raised in Nazareth.

The family remained in Egypt until the death of Herod. Herod died at sixty-nine years of age in March of 4 BC, at his palace in Jericho.[9] The despot knew no tears would be shed at his death, so he ordered the execution of many significant Jewish people when he died, thus there would be weeping instead of celebrating. Fortunately, the order was revoked by Herod's sister when he died.[10]

After Herod's death, an angel of the Lord appeared to Joseph in a dream and instructed him to "get up, take the child and his mother, and go to the land of Israel, because those who intended to kill the child are dead" (vv. 19–20). Joseph responded with prompt obedience; he "got up, took the child and his mother, and entered the land of Israel" (v. 21). The angel's message did not specifically tell Joseph where to go. Matthew provides the distinct impression that Joseph intended to return to Bethlehem. However, once again through a dream, God directed Joseph to take his family to Galilee rather than to Judea. The reason for this was that Herod's son "Archelaus was ruling over Judea in place of his father Herod" (v. 22).

After Herod the Great's death, his kingdom was divided among three sons. Herod Archelaus was appointed as the ethnarch

---

[9] Wilkins, *Matthew*, ZIBC, 18.
[10] Wilkins, *Matthew*, ZIBC, 18.

(ruler) over Judea, Samaria, and Idumea. Archelaus was a brutal and oppressive person, much like his father. The Roman government deposed him in AD 6 and handed his territory over to direct Roman control. Herod Philip was given the predominantly Gentile areas east and north of the Sea of Galilee. Philip was the half-brother of Archelaus and Antipas. Herod Antipas was appointed ruler over Galilee. Antipas was the younger brother of Archelaus. Jesus grew up and carried out much of his ministry in Antipas's territory. Antipas was responsible for the execution of John the Baptist after John criticized him for the unlawful marriage to his brother's wife (Mark 6:14–29). Later when Antipas heard about the miracles Jesus was performing, he thought Jesus might be John the Baptist come back from the dead (Luke 9:7–9). Jesus would later refer to Antipas by the derogatory term "fox" (Luke 13:32). During the final hours of Jesus's life, Pilate sent Jesus to Antipas. Jesus refused to speak a word to him (Luke 23:6–12).[11]

Matthew understood Jesus's family's return to Nazareth (*Nazaret*) to be the fulfillment of Scripture: "he would be called a Nazarene" (*Nazōraios*) (v. 23). Why would Jesus be called "a Nazarene"? In the ancient world, people did not have last names. To differentiate people with the same first name from one another, a qualifying designation like "the Nazarene" was added as a distinguishing indicator. This prophecy is perplexing in that it does not match any prophecy in the Bible. Scholars generally understand Matthew's reference in one of two ways. First, some see the key to understanding this prophecy to be Matthew's use of the plural "prophets," instead of the singular "prophet"

---

[11] For a full discussion see Helen K. Bond, "Herodian Dynasty," in *Dictionary of Jesus and the Gospels*, ed. Joel B. Green, 2nd ed. (Downers Grove: IVP Academic, 2013), 379–82.

as elsewhere in his Birth and Infancy narrative (1:22; 2:5, 15, 17).[12] What does Matthew intend his readers to understand by his use of the plural "prophets"? Nazareth was an obscure and insignificant village in Jesus's day. When Philip told Nathaniel they had found the Messiah, Jesus of Nazareth, Nathaniel said, "Can anything good come out of Nazareth" (John 1:46). How could the Messiah be from such an insignificant village? The use of the plural "prophets" could point to a theme running through the prophetic literature that the Messiah would be despised and rejected, much like a person from Nazareth. Two passages from Isaiah offer examples supporting this thought.

> "Just as many were appalled at you—
> his appearance was so disfigured
> that he did not look like a man,
> and his form did not resemble a human being." (Isa
>   52:14)

> He grew up before him like a young plant
> and like a root out of dry ground.
> He didn't have an impressive form
> Or majesty that we should look at him,
> no appearance that we should desire him.
> He was despised and rejected by men,
> a man of suffering who knew what sickness was.
> He was like someone people turned away from;
> he was despised, and we didn't value him.
> Yet he himself bore our sicknesses,
> and he carried our pains;
> but we in turn regarded him stricken,

---

[12] Blomberg, *Matthew*, 70.

struck down by God, and afflicted.

But he was pierced because of our rebellion,
Crushed because of our iniquities;
punishment for our peace was on him,
and we are healed by his wounds.
We all went astray like sheep;
We all have turned to our own way;
and the LORD has punished him for the iniquity of us all.
He was oppressed and afflicted,
yet he did not open his mouth.
Like a lamb led to the slaughter
and like a sheep silent before her shearers,
he did not open his mouth.
He was taken away because of oppression and judgment,
and who considered his fate?
For he was cut off from the land of the living;
he was struck because of my people's rebellion.
He was assigned a grave with the wicked,
but he was with a rich man at his death,
because he had done no violence
and had not spoken deceitfully. (Isa 53:2–9)

Most Jewish people expected the Messiah to come from Bethlehem. Although Jesus was born in Bethlehem, he was known as Jesus of Nazareth.

A second understanding of the passage focuses on a play on the Hebrew word "branch" (*netzer*) and its similarity to the word Nazareth (*Nazōraios*).[13] If this is Matthew's point, then he is highlighting Jesus as the "branch of Jesse." The key passage

---

[13] Blomberg, *Matthew*, 70.

reads, "Then a shoot will spring from the stem of Jesse, and a
Branch from his roots will bear fruit. The Spirit of the LORD
will rest on Him" (Isa 11:1–2 NASB). Wilkins rightly notes
the possibility of a double meaning, incorporating both aspects
discussed above.[14] Therefore, considering Isa 11:1, Matthew
highlights Jesus's descent from David and, at the same time, the
relative obscurity of one coming from Nazareth. Wilkins suggests that, by the reference to Nazareth, Matthew foreshadows
both Jesus's obscurity and ultimate rejection, despite being the
shoot from Jessie![15]

Final Reflections

Two main thoughts will be examined in this section. First,
Matthew introduces the idea that Jesus is the new and greater
Moses.[16] Moses was born in Egypt under a sentence of death.
Pharaoh had ordered all Hebrew baby boys to be killed (Exod
1:15–16). Moses's mother protected him until she could no
longer keep his gender a secret. She then placed him in a basket and lowered the basket into the Nile where he was discovered by Pharaoh's daughter (Exod 2:1–8). After Moses killed
an Egyptian, he was sentenced to death by Pharaoh (Exod
2:11–15). Moses eventually returned and led the Hebrews
out of Egypt. Like Moses, Jesus was born under a threat of

---

[14] Michael J. Wilkins, *Matthew: From Biblical Text to Contemporary
Life*, NIV Application Commentary (Grand Rapids: Zondervan, 2004), 119.

[15] Wilkins, *Matthew*, NIVAC, 119.

[16] Grant Osborne states that "at nearly every point of the plot in
chs. 1–2, this Moses typology is evident." See Grant Osborne, *Matthew*,
Zondervan Exegetical Commentary on the New Testament (Grand
Rapids: Zondervan, 2010), 101.

death by the orders of Herod the Great. Just as Moses led the Hebrews out of Egypt, Jesus will lead his people out of bondage to Satan, sin, and death. While Moses was the inaugurator of the old covenant, Jesus inaugurates a new covenant. Further evidence that Matthew intends to portray Jesus as a new and greater Moses is that Matthew's Gospel is organized around five of Jesus's sermons (5–7; 10:5–42; 13:1–52; 18; and 23–25). These five sermons correspond loosely with Moses's five books of the Pentateuch. As Jesus went up on a mountain to give the Sermon on the Mount, so Moses went up on Mount Sinai to receive God's law. In addition, when you consider the miracle of Jesus feeding the five thousand (Matt 14:13–21) and walking on the water (Matt 14:22–33) with Moses's feeding Israel and parting the Red Sea, the comparison seems even clearer. Finally, God told Moses, "I will raise up for them a prophet like you from among their brothers. I will put my words in his mouth, and he will tell them everything I command him" (Deut 18:18).

The author of Hebrews understood Jesus to be greater than Moses when he wrote:

> Therefore, holy brothers and sisters, who share in a heavenly calling, consider Jesus, the apostle and high priest of our confession. He was faithful to the one who appointed him, just as Moses was in all God's household. For Jesus is considered worthy of more glory than Moses, just as the builder has more honor than the house. Now every house is built by someone, but the one who built everything is God. Moses was faithful as a servant in all God's household, as a testimony to what would be said in the future. But Christ was faithful as a Son over his household. And

we are that household if we hold on to our confidence and the hope in which we boast. (Heb 3:1–6)

Although Moses was a picture of a better Savior to come, Moses fell short. Moses sinned and did not enter the Promised Land. Jesus did not sin but instead died for sinners (1 Cor 15:3). Jesus truly is greater than Moses.

A second thought on this passage must focus on Herod the Great's attempt to kill the baby Jesus. The apostle John pulls back the curtain on this event and allows his readers to understand that the attempt on Jesus's life was satanic in origin. Revelation 12:1–5 reads:

> A great sign appeared in heaven: a woman clothed with the sun, with the moon under her feet and a crown of twelve stars on her head. She was pregnant and cried out in labor and agony as she was about to give birth. Then another sign appeared in heaven: There was a great fiery red dragon having seven heads and ten horns, and on its heads were seven crowns. Its tail swept away a third of the stars in heaven and hurled them to the earth. And the dragon stood in front of the woman who was about to give birth, so that when she did give birth it might devour her child. She gave birth to a Son, a male who is going to rule all nations with an iron rod. Her child was caught up to God and to his throne.

The apocalyptic nature of the passage is strange to contemporary readers. John is giving his readers insight into the meaning of earthly events in the life of Christ and the church. The chapter opens with a description of a lovely and exalted woman, clothed with the radiance of the sun. Initially, one may think the image depicts Mary; however, the description is far too great to describe a single woman.[17] Rather, the imagery represents the messianic community from which the Messiah will come. The thought of God's people depicted as a woman is a common thought in Revelation and the Old Testament (Isa 54:5; Jer 3:8–9; Rev 19:7–9). Clearly, the great red dragon and the fallen stars symbolize Satan and his demons. Herod's attempt to kill Jesus is represented by the imagery of Satan waiting for the woman to give birth so that he may devour her child. John helps us understand that what took place with the murder of the children was nothing short of a satanic attempt to kill Jesus, the newborn King of the Jews. Behind the scenes of human history there was much taking place in the spiritual world that the human world knew nothing about.

A Christmas Hymn of Response

It came upon the midnight clear,
That glorious song of old,
From angels bending near the earth
To touch their harps of gold:
"Peace on the earth, good will to men,"
From heaven's all-gracious King.
The world in solemn stillness lay,
To hear the angels sing.

Still through the cloven skies they come
with peaceful wings unfurled,

---

[17] Thomas R. Schreiner, "Revelation," in *Hebrews–Revelation*, vol. 12, ed. Iain M. Duguid, James M. Hamilton, Jr., and Jay Sklar, ESV Expository Commentary (Wheaton, IL: Crossway, 2018), 659–61.

and still their heavenly music floats
o'er all the weary world;
above its sad and lowly plains,
they bend on hovering wing,
and ever o'er its Babel sounds
the blessed angels sing.

All ye, beneath life's crushing load,
Whose forms are bending low,
Who toil along the climbing way
With painful steps and slow,
Look now! for glad and golden hours
Come swiftly on the wing:
O rest beside the weary road,
And hear the angels sing!

For lo! the days are hast'ning on,
By prophet bands foretold,
When with the ever-circling years
Comes round the age of gold;
When peace shall over all the earth
Its ancient splendors fling,
And the whole world give back the song
Which now the angels sing.[18]

---

[18] Edmund H. Sears, "It Came upon the Midnight Clear," 1849, *Baptist Hymnal*, #93.

CHAPTER 13

THE CHILDHOOD OF JESUS: THE SIGN OF THINGS TO COME

LUKE 2:41–52

> "Didn't you know that it was necessary
> for me to be in my Father's house?"
> —Luke 2:49

This is the only account in the Bible of an event between Jesus's infancy and adulthood. These events took place approximately a decade following the family's flight to Egypt and their return to Nazareth. While this awkward situation did not technically occur during Jesus's infancy, the passage is still considered within the larger context of Luke's Birth and Infancy narrative. The present passage has much to say about Jesus's incarnation and his understanding of his relationship with his heavenly Father. In this passage, the material related to Jesus's infancy has already taken place. Jesus was on the verge of becoming a young man.

The passage is not intended to cast a bad light on Joseph and Mary but to reveal that Jesus was very much aware of his relationship to his heavenly Father. An additional purpose in the passage is to complete the contrast with John the Baptist. The final comments concerning John the Baptist describe him as growing physically and becoming "strong in spirit" (1:80). Jesus, on the other hand, is described as growing "in wisdom and stature, and in favor with God and with people" (v. 52). Jesus's superiority to John is seen through Luke's description of John maturing in two areas compared to Jesus's growth in four areas: physical, intellectual, spiritual, and social. These aspects of Jesus's maturity will be described later in this chapter. These "silent" years were a favorite for apocryphal Gospels to recount erroneous events in Jesus's childhood.[1]

A Parental Oversight (2:41–48)

Jesus's parents made an annual journey to Jerusalem to celebrate the Passover festival (v. 41). Passover was one of three Jewish pilgrimage festivals and commemorated God's rescue of the Hebrew people from Egyptian bondage (Exod 23:14–17). While the law required only Jewish men to attend the three great pilgrimage festivals, Joseph and the entire family traveled to Jerusalem on this occasion. The journey from Nazareth to Jerusalem would have taken three to four days. A day's journey could be as far as twenty to twenty-five miles.[2] Families made substantial sacrifices

---

[1] For example, see Oscar Cullmann, "The Protevangelium of James," in *New Testament Apocrypha*, ed. Wilhelm Schneemelcher, trans. Robert McLachlan Wilson, rev. ed., 2 vols. (Louisville: Westminster John Knox, 1990).

[2] Robert H. Stein, *Luke*, vol. 24, The New American Commentary (Nashville: B&H Academic, 1992), 121.

to attend Passover. For example, many men in first-century Israel worked as artisans or farmers. Those who worked as farmers still needed someone to care for the crops. Shepherds needed someone to tend their sheep. The idea of paid vacation was foreign to the ancient world. Throughout much of human history, if a person did not work, they did not get paid. A family often left behind others to tend their livestock and work in their fields. This is one reason why only the husband would attend the festival while the remainder of the family would stay behind.

Jesus and his family must have been filled with excitement as they entered the holy city through one of the many gates. The family may have been met by as many as 200,000 people, and the city would be abuzz as vendors and merchants lined the streets. Luke does not describe Jesus celebrating another Passover until the one shortly before his death. Passover proper was the first day of a seven-day (or eight-day) celebration combined with the Feast of Unleavened Bread. The entire festival was often referred to as the Feast of Passover.

Jesus was twelve years old when they made this journey to Jerusalem (v. 42). Earl Ellis understands the reference to Jesus's age as indicating the trip was in some way connected to his *bar mitzvah* ("son of the commandment").[3] At thirteen years of age, a Jewish boy entered the full responsibilities of adulthood.[4] During the preceding year, the father was required to acquaint his son with the duties and responsibilities of manhood. R. T. France,

---

[3] E. Earl Ellis, *The Gospel of Luke*, rev. ed., New Century Bible Commentary (Grand Rapids: Eerdmans, 1974), 85. Also see Craig S. Keener, *The IVP Bible Background Commentary: New Testament* (Downers Grove: IVP Academic, 1993), 199.

[4] Darrell L. Bock, *Luke*, Baker Exegetical Commentary on the New Testament, 2 vols. (Grand Rapids: Baker Academic, 1994), 1:264.

however, notes that no evidence exists for a *bar mitzvah* ceremony until hundreds of years later. Furthermore, France finds it hard to believe that Luke would not mention such an important ceremony considering his earlier description of Jesus's parents fulfilling other significant ceremonies (cf. vv. 21–24).[5] Although the ceremony of the Jewish *bar mitzvah* may not have been in practice at that time, Luke's reference to Jesus's age as more than just chronological is not inconceivable, especially considering Jesus's comment to his mother. Therefore, as Jesus transitions from boyhood to manhood, he makes clear he is cognizant of his relationship to his heavenly Father, and this seems to be the major point of the passage.

By some unexplained mix-up, Jesus is left behind in Jerusalem (vv. 43–44). This perplexing situation leads to many questions the text does not answer. For example, how could Jesus have been left alone in Jerusalem? Did Jesus stay behind intentionally? Why was Mary so confused by Jesus's answer to her question (v. 49)? Where did Jesus stay during those days? Should any specific thought be attached to the fact that the event transpired over a three-day period, since this is the same amount of time Jesus's body lay in the tomb? The text does not answer these questions for us; but as Joseph and Mary's oldest son, he was likely quite resourceful and more than capable of caring for himself for this brief period. The fact that people traveled in caravans from villages like Nazareth for protection from robbers may explain the mix-up of Jesus being left behind.[6] The men and women may have walked in groups separately with the

---

[5] R. T. France, *Luke*, Teach the Text Commentary Series (Grand Rapids: Baker Books, 2013), 44.

[6] Keener, *IVP Bible Background*, 195.

children free to roam among them. If this were the case, then Mary and Joseph may have thought Jesus was with others in their party.[7]

One should not attribute sin to Jesus, regardless of how the question is answered as to why Jesus remained behind in Jerusalem. The New Testament is clear that Jesus never sinned. Paul affirmed the sinlessness of Jesus when he described Jesus as one "who knew no sin" (2 Cor 5:21 NASB). Jesus would later say to his enemies, "Who among you can convict me of sin?" (John 8:46). Jesus lived in complete obedience to his heavenly Father, always doing what was pleasing to him (John 8:29). For one to say Jesus sinned because he remained behind in Jerusalem contradicts the clear teaching of Scripture.

At the end of the first day, Joseph and Mary discovered that Jesus was missing. They must have been frantic when they learned that Jesus was not with the caravan. At daybreak, the troubled parents promptly returned to Jerusalem to search for Jesus, but the return trip was an entire day's journey (v. 45). "On the third day" (counting from the day they left, the day's journey back, and one day looking for him), they find him in the temple (*hieros*) conversing with the religious teachers (*didaskaloi*) (vv. 46–47). The mention of "three days" should not be understood as pointing to Jesus's resurrection, since Luke used the expression "on the third day" to refer to Jesus's resurrection (9:22; 18:33; 24:7, 21, 46).[8] Luke uses the word "teachers" to refer to Jesus's dialogue partners instead of his regular terms "lawyers" (*nomikos*) and "scribes" (*grammateus*), putting the conversation in

---

[7] Bock, *Luke*, 1:266.

[8] Stein, *Luke*, 122. David E. Garland, *Luke*, Zondervan Exegetical Commentary on the New Testament (Grand Rapids: Zondervan, 2011), 144.

a more positive light. Luke uses the terms "lawyers" and "scribes" in a negative light throughout the Gospel.[9]

Often rabbinic teaching sessions took the form of question-and-answer interactions.[10] Those listening to Jesus were "astounded" (*existēmi*) by the wisdom and insight of one so young (v. 47). Isaiah 11:2 is a messianic text that reflects on the keen insight the Messiah would possess: "The Spirit of the LORD will rest on him—a Spirit of wisdom and understanding, a Spirit of counsel and strength, a Spirit of knowledge and of the fear of the LORD."

Joseph and Mary must have been quite frustrated with Jesus when they eventually found him. Mary seemingly puts the blame for the confusion squarely on Jesus, "Son, why have you treated us like this? Your father and I have been anxiously searching for you" (v. 48). The reference to Joseph as Jesus's father should be understood in consideration of earlier passages. One might wonder why Mary would have expressed such frustration with Jesus after all she had been told about him by the angels and shepherds. Several thoughts come to mind. First, there is no evidence that their family was any different than any other family. The biblical text's silence seems to indicate a certain normalcy for the family during these "silent years." Neither Luke nor Matthew record any supernatural appearances by angels or prophetic words by godly individuals concerning Jesus; thus, we are left with the impression that their lives were rather normal. Second, like any other mother, Mary would have been desperate to find her missing son, and her anxiety spilled over into her seemingly stern words to Jesus. Third, we must never forget that Mary herself

---

[9] Mark L. Strauss, *Luke*, Zondervan Illustrated Bible Backgrounds Commentary (Grand Rapids: Zondervan, 2002), 33.

[10] Strauss, *Luke*, 33.

was a sinner. Although a woman of great faith and devotion, she still needed a savior.

Jesus's "First Words" (2:49–52)

We know nothing about what Jesus said for the first twelve years of his life until this moment, and nothing after these words until he is in his early thirties. For Luke, this exchange between Mary and Jesus must have been monumentally important. Why else would Luke choose to recount this single exchange? Jesus's response to Mary's question is most surprising. His answer implies Mary should have known he would be "in his Father's house." The word for "house" is not in the Greek text. (Hence, the KJV rendering, "about my Father's business.") A word must be added based upon the context to make sense of the statement in English. The context favors the interpretation of Jesus's statement as being a reference to his location ("house") rather than to his activity.[11]

What is even more impressive than Jesus's interaction with the teachers is his awareness of his relationship with his heavenly Father (v. 49). Jesus's response to Mary stands in sharp contrast to her statement to him, "Your father and I" (v. 48). Jesus turns the attention of the conversation from them to his heavenly Father. Jesus's statement, "It was necessary (*dei*) for me to be in my Father's house" communicates the thought of divine providence. Jesus *had to* be there. Where else would he possibly be?

Luke makes clear, however, that Jesus lived in submission to his earthly parents. He lived in obedience to his own

---

[11] Scholars debate precisely what word to supply for the verse. See Bock, *Luke*, 1:269–270, and Stein, *Luke*, 123.

commandment, "Honor your father and mother" (Exod 20:12; cf. Eph 6:2). Jesus matured much as other boys his age matured. He grew in wisdom (intellectually), stature (physically), in favor with God (spiritually), and in favor with man (socially) (cf. 1 Sam 2:26).[12]

While contemplating God in human flesh is astonishing, to think the incarnate omniscient Savior had to grow in his understanding of Scripture is equally amazing. Isaiah prophesied that the Messiah would become wise by listening to the words of Scripture. "The Lord GOD has given me the tongue of those who are instructed to know how to sustain the weary with a word. He awakens me each morning; he awakens my ear to listen like those being instructed. The Lord GOD has opened my ear, and I was not rebellious; I did not turn back" (Isa 50:4–5). Jesus's parents must have faithfully taught him the Scriptures and raised him regularly attending synagogue worship. The wisdom Jesus demonstrated by his interactions with the teachers is reminiscent of Ps 119:99–100: "I have more insight than all my teachers because your [God] decrees are my meditation. I understand more than the elders because I obey your [God] precepts." The admiration of the teachers would be relatively short-lived. The descendants of these teachers who were so impressed by Jesus would one day call for his crucifixion. Rather than learn from his divine wisdom and insight, they would grow to hate him.

Luke mentions for a second time that Mary "kept all these things in her heart" (v. 51; 2:19). While Mary may not have fully

---

[12] Raymond E. Brown, *The Birth of the Messiah: A Commentary on the Infancy Narratives in Matthew and Luke* (Garden City, NY: Doubleday, 1977), 483; Brown warns against making too much of this phrase to determine Jesus's level of self-awareness.

grasped the full implications of Jesus's statement about having to be in his Father's house, she did not forget those words. Luke may be indicating that Mary was the source of this information. Even more, she treasured the precious memories of those days and stored them away.

Final Reflections

As always, the most important truths in this passage are Christological. Before we turn to a significant Christological insight, there are a few other key implications for Christian living suggested by this passage. First, Joseph and Mary are presented once again as a model couple. They were certainly not perfect people, and they did not have a perfect marriage (no one does), but we find them making the wise decision to worship God at the Passover in Jerusalem. The journey from Nazareth to Jerusalem took several days. Luke indicates they did this "every year." From the information we have about this couple, Scripture points to the practice of keeping their priorities in order. Passionate devotion to God characterized their home from the beginning. Twelve years after the ceremonies described in Luke 2:21–24, they are still demonstrating faithfulness to God. Jesus's earthly parents were not just theologically orthodox but also genuinely pious. The two qualities are not always found together. During the busyness of life, other things can easily crowd out heartfelt love for God. Current studies reveal that college-age adults are leaving the church at an alarming rate. Sometimes parents point the finger at the church, but they should consider whether their choices during their children's crucial teenage years placed priority either on the eternal or on the temporal in their family life.

Obviously, Joseph and Mary lived in a much different age from ours, but every age has unique challenges. The challenges of the modern age—24/7 access to social media and the rapid decline of moral and sexual standards, to name just two—make parental involvement in their children's spiritual lives more important than ever. The world looks innocuous, harmless, and even enticing, but it is seeking to seduce us and our children into a dark, godless place. So what do we do? Do we hide our children away? Do we barricade ourselves in our homes? No, we do not hide ourselves away, but we must seek to keep our eye on the ball—raising our children in the nurture and admonition of the Lord (Eph 6:4). We must quit playing games with our own spiritual lives and make godly, Christ-honoring choices. Parents must beware of the distraction of the good. For example, there are many activities our children can and should be involved in as they grow up, but making sure those activities don't keep children from church is of paramount importance. Examine your family life and ask if your children's spiritual lives are a high priority. Ask yourself if they see you as the same person at home as you are at church. Pray fervently for your children, love them deeply, and guide them intentionally. Cast off passionless religiosity, and seek God wholeheartedly yourself. Stop making the same excuses you have made for years for your spiritual lethargy. Parenting is a gift and a great responsibility. What little we know about the family life of Joseph and Mary points to their devotion to God.

Christian teenagers have much to learn from their incarnate Lord, as well. Although Jesus knew himself to be the Son of God, he lived in submission to his earthly parents. If the religious teachers were impressed by his wisdom and insight at the age of twelve, before long his knowledge of Scripture would surpass that of his parents. Yet Jesus returned to Nazareth and lived in a way that demonstrated honor and respect to his parents. When teenagers honor and respect their parents, they demonstrate honor and respect for God. The more teenagers (and children) love Jesus, the more they will prove that love by how they treat their parents. Let me speak directly to teenagers at this point. Do not only obey your parents but seek to be a blessing to them. Do your chores with a glad heart. Look for ways to bless them by helping them. Speak kindly and graciously to them and about them to others. Show your love for Jesus by loving your parents well.

As impressive as the example of Mary and Joseph is in this passage, Jesus is even more remarkable. Much of Jesus's life was lived out of the limelight. From his infancy until his early thirties, we know of only one event in Jesus's life. We know of only a few words spoken by him during that same period. One who was so great and glorious went about his daily mundane existence, performing his chores without attracting much attention. Although he understood perfectly well his unique relationship to God the Father, he lived in full submission to his earthly parents. This obedience demonstrates unimaginable humility. As Paul wrote, Jesus is one "who, existing in the form of God, did not consider equality with God as something to be exploited. Instead he emptied himself by assuming the form of a servant, taking on the likeness of humanity" (Phil 2:6–7). Jesus attracted no attention to himself. Later, as he began to reveal slowly his true identity by his miracles, some would say, "Isn't this Jesus the son of Joseph, whose father and mother we know? How can he now say, 'I have come down from heaven'?" (John 6:42). Jesus knew who he was and had a powerful ability to perform miracles at his disposal, yet he lived a godly life during his early life in a small Galilean village. Pastors and those aspiring to pastoral ministry would do well to reflect on Jesus's example. Who we are as we live *backstage* will determine to a great extent who we will be when God allows us to lead his people. Those training for ministry should never despise the "silent years." There is much to learn and much growth that needs to take place there. A longing for recognition must be faced during the silent years. God has much to accomplish in our lives before God entrusts leadership of his people into our care. If we will not live in the shadows for God's glory, we do not deserve the privilege of leading God's people. Jesus submitted himself to those he created. The depth of Jesus's humility is staggering. One who had been worshiped by the angels lived in submission to his earthly parents.

A Christmas Hymn of Response

O little town of Bethlehem,
How still we see thee lie!
Above thy deep and dreamless sleep
The silent stars go by;
Yet in thy dark streets shineth
The everlasting Light;
The hopes and fears of all the years
Are met in thee tonight.

For Christ is born of Mary,
And gathered all above,
While mortals sleep, the angels keep
Their watch of wondering love.

O morning stars, together
Proclaim the holy birth,
And praises sing to God the King,

And peace to men on earth!

O little town of Bethlehem
How still we see thee lie
Above thy deep and dreamless sleep
The silent stars go by
Yet in thy dark streets shineth
The everlasting light
The hopes and fears of all the years
Are met in thee tonight.[13]

---

[13] Philip Brooks, "O Little Town of Bethlehem," 1868, *Baptist Hymnal,* #86.

CHAPTER 14

THE OLD TESTAMENT MESSIANIC EXPECTATION OF A COMING ONE

> "I will put hostility between you and the woman,
> and between your offspring and her offspring.
> He will strike your head,
> and you will strike his heel."
> —Genesis 3:15

G od's announcement of Christ's coming did not begin with Gabriel's visit to Mary. The announcement of God's plan was first made known in the garden of Eden. After Adam and Eve's fall into sin, God made known his intentions to redeem a people for himself. Beginning with the *protoevangelium* (Gen 3:15), the Old Testament points toward a Coming One. God said to the serpent, "I will put hostility between you and the woman, and between your offspring and her offspring. *He* will strike your head, and you will strike *his* heel" (italics added). From that point forward in redemptive history, God was preparing the world for the coming of his beloved Son, Jesus the Messiah (Gal 4:4).

As we trace the Messianic hope in the Old Testament, we will focus attention most closely on Abraham, Moses, and David because of their significance. These three individuals are the Mount Rushmore of the Old Testament, and their names appeared often in our study of the Birth and Infancy narratives. Additionally, we will briefly explore key prophecies in Isaiah that help round out our understanding of the kind of Messiah Jesus would be.[1] Before we begin our examination of select Old Testament texts, the first-century context of Jewish Messianic expectations will be explained briefly.

First-Century Jewish Messianic Expectation

Jewish hopes of the coming Messiah in Jesus's day were not monolithic.[2] The most prevalent view, however, was that the Messiah would be a warrior-king, like David. The Jewish people considered themselves to be in exile. Even though the Babylonian exile had ended centuries prior, they found themselves under the heavy hand of Roman domination. The Jewish people longed for messianic freedom. An example of

---

[1] My thoughts on "Jesus in the Old Testament" have been shaped by the following authors: T. D. Alexander, *The Servant King: The Bible's Portrait of the Messiah* (Vancouver, BC: Regent College, 2003); Walter C. Kaiser, Jr., *The Messiah in the Old Testament* (Grand Rapids: Zondervan, 1995); Thomas R. Schreiner, *Covenant and God's Purpose for the World*, Short Studies in Biblical Theology (Wheaton, IL: Crossway, 2017); Christopher J. H. Wright, *Knowing Jesus Through the Old Testament* (Downers Grove: IVP Academic, 1992).

[2] For a discussion on this topic see Michael F. Bird, *Are You the One Who Is to Come? The Historical Jesus and the Messianic Question* (Grand Rapids: Baker Academic, 2009), esp. 31–62; Joseph A. Fitzmyer, *The One Who Is to Come* (Grand Rapids: Eerdmans, 2007); Wright, *Knowing Jesus*, 137–40.

this hope can be found in the *Psalms of Solomon*, a pseudepigraphic ("falsely inscribed") work from the first century BC. The following is a representative passage from the Psalms of Solomon 17:21–25.

> See, Lord, and raise up for them their king, the son of
>   David, to rule over your servant Israel . . .
> Undergird him with the strength to destroy the unrighteous rulers;
> to purge Jerusalem from Gentiles who trample her to
>   destruction;
> in wisdom and in righteousness to drive out the sinners
>   from the inheritance;
> to smash the arrogance of sinners like a potter's jar;
> to shatter all their substance with an iron rod;
> to destroy unlawful nations with the sword of his mouth;
> and he will condemn sinners by the thoughts of their
>   hearts.[3]

This revolutionary theme can be found in Mary's *Magnificat* (Luke 1:46–55) and Zechariah's *Benedictus* (Luke 1:68–79).

The Expectations of a Coming One in the Old Testament

As mentioned above, we will focus on three key figures (Abraham, Moses, and David) as well as one significant Old Testament prophet (Isaiah).

---

[3] W. B. Wright, "Psalms of Solomon: A New Translation and Introduction," in *The Old Testament Pseudepigrapha*, ed. J. H. Charlesworth, 2 vols. (Garden City, NY: Doubleday, 1985), 2:667.

The Seed of Abraham

After God's reference to the "seed of the woman" in Genesis 3, the next substantial advance in the messianic storyline is God's covenant with Abraham.[4] God promised Abraham that through "his seed" all the nations of the earth would be blessed. As we have seen earlier, the key texts are Gen 12:1–3 and Gen 22:15–18. These texts are printed below.

> The LORD said to Abram:
> Go from your land,
> your relatives,
> and your father's house
> to the land that I will show you.
> I will make you into a great nation,
> I will bless you,
> I will make your name great,
> and you will be a blessing.
> I will bless those who bless you,
>
> I will curse anyone who treats you with contempt, and all the peoples on earth will be blessed through you. (Gen 12:1–3)
>
> Then the angel of the LORD called to Abraham a second time from heaven and said, "By myself I have sworn," this is the LORD's declaration: "Because you have done this thing and have not withheld your only son, I will

---

[4] See Trent Hunter and Stephen J. Wellum, *Christ from Beginning to End: How the Full Story of Scripture Reveals the Full Glory of God* (Grand Rapids: Zondervan, 2018), 112–27. In addition, see Schreiner, *Covenant and God's Purpose for the World*, 41–57.

indeed bless you and make your offspring as numerous as the stars of the sky and the sand on the seashore. Your offspring will possess the city gates of their enemies. And all the nations of the earth will be blessed by your offspring because you have obeyed my command." (Gen 22:15–18)

The apostle Paul makes clear that the ultimate reference to the promised seed of Abraham is Jesus Christ: "Now the promises were spoken to Abraham and to his seed. He does not say 'and to seeds,' as though referring to many, but referring to one, and to your seed, who is Christ" (Gal 3:16). Paul goes on to say in the same passage, "And if you belong to Christ, then you are Abraham's seed, heirs according to the promise" (Gal 3:29).

Abraham is a monumental figure in the Old Testament. It is no exaggeration to say that the fulfillment of these promises to Abraham is at the heart of redemptive history.[5] God's promise to Abraham to bless the nations through his seed is central to worldwide evangelization.[6] God's covenant with Abraham *implies* both a command and a promise. The gospel is to be taken to all nations, and all the nations of the world will be blessed through the One to whom the gospel points: Jesus the Messiah.

Before we leave Abraham, we will briefly explore his immediate descendants and their role in the developing story. The next one in the Messianic story line is Abraham's son, Isaac. Although Isaac was not Abraham's firstborn son (Ishmael was), Isaac was the child of promise (Gen 17:19). In one of the most dramatic moments in redemptive history, Abraham was prepared to offer

---

[5] Wright, *Knowing Jesus*, 83.
[6] Wright, 83.

Isaac as a sacrificial offering to God, but God redeemed Isaac with the substitute of a ram (Gen 22:10–18). While Abraham did not sacrifice his firstborn son, God did sacrifice his only Son, who died as a substitute for sinners. Later, God reaffirmed to Isaac the promise he had made to his father Abraham, "I will make your offspring as numerous as the stars of the sky, I will give your offspring all these lands, and all the nations of the earth will be blessed by your offspring" (Gen 26:4).

Isaac became the father of two sons—Esau and Jacob. Jacob was the son through whom the messianic promise would be passed along. Although Jacob inherited the family trait of deception, God eventually changed his name to Israel. Abraham, Isaac, and Jacob become the three patriarchal names most often mentioned together in the Old Testament. From Jacob, the messianic line goes through Judah. However, Judah's brother Joseph also fills a crucial role in the messianic storyline.[7]

Although Joseph is not a biological descendant of Judah, he plays a major role in Genesis (37, 39–50). In many ways, Joseph foreshadows several key events in Jesus's life. For example, Joseph is despised and hated by his brothers (all sons of Jacob), much as Jesus was hated by many of his own countrymen (John 1:11; 15:18–21). Joseph was taken to Egypt, as was Jesus (Gen 39; Matt 2:14–15). Just as Jesus prayed for the forgiveness of those crucifying him, Joseph forgave his brothers for their betrayal of him (Luke 23:34; Gen 50:15–21). In a very real sense, God used Joseph to *save* Israel (Jacob) and his family from starvation by bringing them to Egypt. In a much more glorious way, Jesus saves his people from their sins (Matt 1:21).

---

[7] Alexander, *Servant King*, 30.

Judah, however, is the one through whom the messianic seed passed. Although Judah convinced his brothers to sell Joseph into slavery (Gen 37:26–27), he later offered himself to Joseph as a substitute slave for Benjamin (Gen 44:18–34). Of all the events associated with Judah, the most important is his father Jacob's blessing.

> The scepter will not depart from Judah
> or the staff from between his feet
> until he whose right it is comes
> and the obedience of the peoples belongs to him. (Gen 49:10)

John the apostle refers to the above passage in Rev 5:5, "Then one of the elders said to me, 'Do not weep. Look, the Lion from the tribe of Judah, the Root of David, has conquered so that he is able to open the scroll and its seven seals.'"

A Prophet Like Moses

As the Old Testament story of the promise continues to unfold, the next major one is Moses. God promised Moses that he would raise up a prophet like him.

> The LORD your God will raise up for you a prophet like me from among your own brothers. You must listen to him. This is what you requested from the LORD your God at Horeb on the day of the assembly when you said, 'Let us not continue to hear the voice of the LORD our God or see this great fire any longer, so that we will not die!' Then the LORD said to me, 'They have spoken well. I will raise up for them a prophet like you

from among their brothers. I will put my words in his mouth, and he will tell them everything I command him. (Deut 18:15–18)

Several key thoughts emerge from this prophecy. First, the prophet to come will speak for God. Second, this coming prophet will come from the Hebrew people. Third, this prophet will be like Moses. John the Baptist alluded to this passage when responding to the religious leaders' question, "Are you *the* Prophet?" (John 1:21, italics added). The religious leaders wanted to know if John considered himself to be the long-anticipated fulfillment of Moses's prophecy. The Baptist not only rejected the idea, but he also informed them that the one who fulfills the prophecy stood among them (John 1:21–28). In Acts, both Peter (3:22) and Stephen (7:37) preached that Jesus fulfilled this Deuteronomic prophecy.

Several other impressive similarities exist between Jesus and Moses. For example, both were inaugurators of a covenant between God and his people—Moses, the old covenant (Exod 34:27), and Jesus, the new covenant (Luke 22:20).[8] Both men were born under dictatorial rulers—Pharaoh and Herod the Great. Both Moses and Jesus were born under the sentence of death (Exodus 2; Matt 2:18–21). Moses spent forty years as a shepherd in the Midian desert (Exod 3:1), while Jesus is the Good Shepherd (John 10:11, 14). Moses performed numerous miracles that Jesus not only replicated but exceeded. For example, the Exodus generation ate manna in the wilderness, but eventually they died. Jesus not only fed thousands with a few pieces of bread and a couple of fish, he also proclaimed that those who eat

---

[8] On the Mosaic covenant, see Schreiner, *Covenant*, 59–72.

the Bread of Life (Jesus) will never die (John 6:31–35). While Moses parted the Red Sea and the children of Israel walked through on dry ground, Jesus walked *on* the Sea of Galilee (Exod 14:15–31; John 6:16–21). While more could be said of the similarities and contrasts between Jesus and Moses, two final comments will have to suffice. First, the author of Hebrews brings out a significant difference between Jesus and Moses.

> He [Jesus] was faithful to the one who appointed him, just as Moses was in all God's household. For Jesus is considered worthy of more glory than Moses, just as the builder has more honor than the house. Now every house is built by someone, but the one who built everything is God. Moses was faithful as a servant in all God's household, as a testimony to what would be said in the future. But Christ was faithful as a Son over his household. And we are that household if we hold on to our confidence and the hope in which we boast. (Heb 3:2–6).

Second, the greatest difference between Moses and Jesus is that Moses not only failed to lead the Israelites into the Promised Land, but he himself did not enter due to his sin (Num 20:12). Jesus, however, has entered heaven and is preparing a place for his followers (John 14:1–2; cf., Revelation 21–22).

A King Like David

The next major one in the Messianic storyline is King David. David was a descendant from the line of Judah. The idea of a coming king goes back as far as Abraham, when God said to Abraham, "I will make you extremely fruitful and will make nations and kings come from you" (Gen 17:6). God made a similar comment to Abraham concerning Sarah, "I will bless her, and she will produce nations; kings of peoples will come from her" (Gen 17:16). The greatest of those kings was David, the former shepherd-boy. Just as God made covenants with Abraham and Moses, God made a covenant with David.[9] The Davidic covenant was a major advance in the Messianic story line. The key passage reads (italics added),

> "When your time comes and you rest with your ancestors, *I will raise up* after you your descendant, who will come from your body, and *I will establish* his kingdom. He is the one who will build a house for my name, and *I will establish* the throne of his kingdom forever. I will be his father, and he will be my son. When he does wrong, *I will discipline him* with a rod of men and blows from mortals. But my faithful love will never leave him as it did when I removed it from Saul, whom I removed from before you. Your house and kingdom will endure before me forever, and your throne will be established forever." (2 Sam 7:12–16)

The covenant consisted of three promises: a hereditary lineage, a kingdom, and a throne (v. 13). The Lord would be a father to David's son, the Lord's representative on the earth (v. 14). If David's descendants turned away from God, they would be punished. God, however, promised never to terminate his covenant with David (vv. 15–16). Although David's descendants sinned against God, the Jewish people clung to the hope of a greater David to come. The angel Gabriel echoed the words of David's covenant when he announced the birth of Jesus, Israel's

---

[9] For a helpful discussion of Davidic covenant, see Schreiner, *Covenant*, 73–87.

long-awaited messianic King (Luke 1:32–33). The connection between David and Jesus is emphasized by Paul in his articulation of the gospel "concerning his Son, Jesus Christ our Lord, who was a descendant of David according to the flesh" (Rom 1:3). Jesus acknowledged himself to be David's son and Lord by quoting Ps 110:1 (Mark 12:35–36).

While Jesus was teaching in the temple, he asked, "How can the scribes say that the Messiah is the son of David? David himself says by the Holy Spirit: The Lord declared to my Lord, 'Sit at my right hand until I put your enemies under your feet'" (Mark 12:35–36). Another key prophecy related to a coming king, which Matthew alludes to in the journey of the wise men, is Num 24:17–19. The importance of Balaam's prophetic words is that when he spoke them, Israel had no king.[10] The text reads,

> I see him, but not now;
> I perceive him, but not near.
> A star will come from Jacob,
> and a scepter will arise from Israel.
> He will smash the forehead of Moab
> and strike down all the Shethites.
> Edom will become a possession;
> Seir will become a possession of its enemies,
> but Israel will be triumphant.
> One who comes from Jacob will rule;
> he will destroy the city's survivors.

Unfortunately, just as Abraham and Moses had significant shortcomings, David also failed to live up to the hopes and expectations of God's people. In David's adulterous relationship with

---

[10] Alexander, *Servant King*, 37.

Bathsheba, he transgressed at least four of the Ten Commandments: murder, adultery, covetousness, and lying (2 Sam 11–12). He also sinned grievously against God by his insistence on the census of his military, demonstrating a sinful hubris in his own military strength (2 Samuel 24). Considering these heinous sins, how could David be described as a man after God's heart (1 Sam 13:14)? I believe we can assume from what David wrote in Psalms 32 and 51 that he genuinely repented from his sins and received God's gracious forgiveness. Perhaps, most important, unlike the kings who followed David, his heart did not chase after false gods, and he remained "fully devoted to the Lord" (1 Kgs 11:4, NIV).

The Servant of the Lord

More than any other prophet, Isaiah paints a comprehensive portrait of the Coming One. Jesus quoted Isa 61:1–2 as a programmatic summary at the beginning of his public ministry (Luke 4:18–19):

> The Spirit of the Lord is on me,
> because he has anointed me
> to preach good news to the poor.
> He has sent me
> to proclaim release to the captives
> and recovery of sight to the blind,
> to set free the oppressed,
> to proclaim the year of the Lord's favor.

In addition, some of the most important messianic markers in the Old Testament are found in what is known as Isaiah's "Servant Songs" (42:1–4; 49:1–6; 50:4–11; and 52:13–53:12). The New Testament authors understood these songs to be fulfilled in Jesus the Messiah. For example, four times in Peter's sermons in the book of Acts, he refers to Jesus as "the servant" (3:13, 26;

4:25, 27). Paul presented Jesus as taking "the very nature of a servant" to the believers at Philippi (Phil 2:7 NIV).

When one considers the Servant Songs in Isaiah, along with information found earlier in the book of Isaiah, the prophet highlights several important features of the Coming One. First, Isaiah establishes an unmistakable link between the Servant and David. For example, the Servant is the ultimate heir to the Davidic throne (9:7; 11:1). The first of these two passages reads, "The dominion will be vast, and its prosperity will never end. He will reign on the throne of David and over his kingdom, to establish and sustain it with justice and righteousness from now on and forever" (Isa 9:7). The second passage is often quoted during the Christmas season: "Then a shoot will grow from the stump of Jesse, and a branch from his roots will bear fruit" (Isa 11:1). Jesse was David's father. In Isa 55:3, the Servant is again identified with David, "Pay attention and come to me; listen, so that you will live. I will make a permanent covenant with you on the basis of the faithful kindnesses of David."

Another feature of Isaiah's portrait of the Servant King is that the servant will be empowered by God's Spirit. The following verses highlight this emphasis (italics added).

> Then a shoot will grow from the stump of Jesse,
> and a branch from his roots will bear fruit.
> The *Spirit* of the LORD will rest on him—
> a *Spirit* of wisdom and understanding,
> a *Spirit* of counsel and strength,
> a *Spirit* of knowledge and of the fear of the LORD.
> His delight will be in the fear of the LORD.
> He will not judge
> by what he sees with his eyes,
> he will not execute justice

by what he hears with his ears,
but he will judge the poor righteously
and execute justice for the oppressed of the land.
He will strike the land
with a scepter from his mouth,
and he will kill the wicked
with a command from his lips. (Isa 11:1–4)

"This is my servant; I strengthen him,
this is my chosen one; I delight in him.
I have put my *Spirit* on him;
he will bring justice to the nations." (Isa 42:1)

Coasts and islands, listen to me;
distant peoples, pay attention.
The LORD called me before I was born.
He named me while I was in my mother's womb.
He made my words like a sharp sword;
he hid me in the shadow of his hand.
He made me like a sharpened arrow;
he hid me in his quiver.
He said to me, "You are my *servant*,
Israel, in whom I will be glorified." (Isa 49:1–3)

The Lord GOD has given me
the tongue of those who are instructed
to know how to sustain the weary with a word.
He awakens me each morning;
he awakens my ear to listen like those being instructed.
    (Isa 50:4)

"As for me, this is my covenant with them," says the
LORD: "My *Spirit* who is on you, and my words that

I have put in your mouth, will not depart from your mouth, or from the mouths of your children, or from the mouths of your children's children, from now on and forever," says the LORD. (Isa 59:21)

The *Spirit* of the Lord GOD is on me,
because the LORD has anointed me
to bring good news to the poor.
He has sent me to heal the brokenhearted,
to proclaim liberty to the captives
and freedom to the prisoners. (Isa 61:1)

A third aspect highlighting the identity of the servant is his identification with God. For example, in Isa 7:14 he is "Immanuel" ("God is with us"). In Isa 9:6, he is called "Mighty God" (9:6). In Isa 53:1, the servant is referred to as the "arm of the Lord." The phrase "arm of the Lord" is used of Yahweh himself in Isa 51:9. The imagery of the "arm of the Lord" suggests God's power and ability to bring about redemption and restoration (Isa 52:10).

Clearly, much more could be written on each of these topics. The amount of material exploring the messianic theme in Scripture is voluminous. The point being made here is that while the coming of Jesus Christ into the world was a surprise to most, the Old Testament foretold of his coming. He didn't come in the manner most first-century Jews expected him to come—as a mighty warrior—but instead he came as the Prince of Peace. Jesus didn't come to establish a Jewish kingdom but the kingdom of God. He was not born in a palace surrounded by dignitaries, but in a stable surrounded by animals. The Coming One came from heaven's throne to Bethlehem's manger.

Final Reflections

Admittedly, our survey of the Old Testament Messianic expectations is brief. The purpose of the chapter was not to provide a detailed analysis of all the evidence but to highlight the fact that from Gen 3:15 onward, God's plan of sending a Savior was being worked out. Certainly, there were long periods of time when God's people struggled to believe God could fulfill his promises. Yet, God's plan unfolded just as he intended, so that in the fullness of time Jesus could be born in the village of Bethlehem, thus fulfilling Mic 5:2. Tracing the prophecies of a Coming One and seeing its fulfillment in the birth of Jesus gives us confidence in God's ability to accomplish all he intends to do. Nothing can stop God's plans. The first Christmas is a reminder to us of God's love and care for his people. Each year when we celebrate Christmas, our hearts should be filled with love and devotion for a God who keeps his promises—every one of them! Christmas is also an invitation for those in the darkness to come into the light of God's Son.

A Christmas Hymn of Response

The First Noel the Angels did say,
Was to certain poor shepherds in fields as they lay;
In fields where they lay keeping their sheep,
On a cold winter's night that was so deep.
Noel Noel Noel Noel
Born is the King of Israel.

For all to see there was a star
Shining in the East, beyond them far,
And to the earth it gave great light,

And so it continued both day and night.
Noel Noel Noel Noel
Born is the King of Israel.

And by the light of that same star
Three Wise men came from country far;
To seek for a King was their intent,
And to follow the star wherever it went.
Noel Noel Noel Noel
Born is the King of Israel.

This star drew nigh to the northwest
O'er Bethlehem it took its rest
And there it did both Pause and stay
Right o'er the place where Jesus lay
Noel Noel Noel Noel

Born is the King of Israel!
Then let us all with one accord
Sing praises to our heavenly Lord
Who hath made heav'n and earth of naught,
And with His blood mankind hath bought.
Noel Noel Noel Noel

Born is the King of Israel.
Noel Noel Noel Noel
Born is the King
Born is the King
Born is the King of Israel![11]

---

[11] Ralph Vaughn Williams, "The First Noel," 1954, *The Baptist Hymnal*, #85.

EPILOGUE

The very first Christmas story began in eternity past. From an earthly perspective the story began in the garden of Eden, when God told the serpent that the seed of the woman would one day crush his head. From that point on, God made promises and covenants with key individuals. At times, the people of God must have thought that those promises would never come to pass. However, when God broke four hundred years of silence by speaking through an angel to Zechariah, and later to Mary, events began to unfold much more quickly. Those events reached a majestic crescendo when an angel told the shepherds, "Today in the city of David a Savior was born for you, who is the Messiah, the Lord. This will be the sign for you: You will find a baby wrapped tightly in cloth and lying in a manger" (Luke 2:11–12). God became flesh and blood and dwelt among us in the person of Jesus the Messiah (John 1:14).

Even though his coming was foretold in the Hebrew Scriptures, no one seemed prepared for Jesus when he arrived. They expected a traditional king, one who was almost certainly a warrior, but they never anticipated a baby. This is just another example of how God has continually confounded the wise and revealed himself to the humble. Those willing to believe the Scriptures and take God at his Word understand his ways are not our ways. The events we have examined demonstrate God's great love for those whom he created. God's willingness to send his Beloved Son to become one of us demonstrates the depth of that love. Those who were there on the night of Jesus's birth (Mary, Joseph, the shepherds, and even the angels) could hardly imagine what lay ahead for that beautiful baby boy. Little did his parents know he "has come to seek and to save the lost" (Luke 19:10), to destroy the works of the devil (1 John 3:8), crush the serpent's head (Gen 3:15), and, ultimately, die for sinners (Rom 5:8). What began in a manger ended with an empty tomb. The manger, the cross, and the empty tomb stand together declaring God's commitment to save us. As I said earlier, for those of you who remain in the darkness, Christmas is God's yearly reminder to come into the light.

NAME AND SUBJECT INDEX

SCRIPTURE INDEX